Quarterly Essay

AF604354

Quarterly Essay is published four times a year by Black Inc., an imprint of Schwartz Books Pty Ltd. Publisher: Morry Schwartz.

ISBN 9781760645021 ISSN 1444-884x

ALL RIGHTS RESERVED.
No part of this publication may be reproduced, stored in a retrieval system, or transmitted in any form by any means electronic, mechanical, photocopying, recording or otherwise without the prior consent of the publishers.

Essay & correspondence © retained by the authors.

Subscriptions – 1 year print & digital (4 issues): $99.99 within Australia incl. GST. Outside Australia $134.99. 1 year digital only: $64.99.

Payment may be made by Mastercard or Visa, or by cheque made out to Schwartz Books. Payment includes postage and handling.

To subscribe, fill out and post the subscription card or form inside this issue, or subscribe online:

quarterlyessay.com
subscribe@quarterlyessay.com
Phone: 61 3 9486 0288

Correspondence should be addressed to:

The Editor, Quarterly Essay
22–24 Northumberland Street
Collingwood VIC 3066 Australia
Phone: 61 3 9486 0288 / Fax: 61 3 9011 6106
Email: quarterlyessay@blackincbooks.com

Editor: Chris Feik. Management: Elisabeth Young. Publicity: Anna Lensky. Design: Guy Mirabella. Associate Editor: Kirstie Innes-Will. Production Coordinator: Marilyn de Castro. Typesetting: Typography Studio.

Printed in Australia by McPherson's Printing Group.

THE GOOD FIGHT

What Does Labor Stand For?

Sean Kelly

Three weeks before the 2025 election, a piece appeared in *The Age* and *The Sydney Morning Herald* under a headline declaring: "This election is one of the worst I've seen." Veteran economic commentator Ross Gittins wrote: "In my 51 years as a journalist, this is the 20th federal election campaign I've observed at close quarters, and I'm convinced they're getting worse: more contrived, manipulative, transactional and misleading, and less focused on the various serious problems facing us, which are far greater than they used to be, and now include America's abdication from leadership of the free world."

A day later, *The Australian*, which for the better part of three years had cheered on the Coalition, ran a piece by foreign affairs commentator Greg Sheridan similarly declaring in the headline that it was the worst campaign he had ever seen. In prim journalese, he wrote, "Here are two once proud teams playing the worst game ever seen to decide the wooden spoon."

Because of the scale of Labor's victory, and because of the influence of Donald Trump – a world-historic figure – this fact now seems forgotten: it was a horribly trivial campaign. Almost nothing of substance was proposed. The sides offered identical health policies, and complete agreement on the nation's most significant foreign policy, AUKUS. Both sides would restrain NDIS spending, reduce international student numbers and ban foreign investors from buying existing homes. On most occasions that gaps threatened to open up, before or during the campaign – on Labor's nature protection laws, on Tasmanian salmon farming, on work from home – they were quickly shut down. An announcement on climate targets, which would certainly have provoked debate, was delayed by Labor until after the poll, as was a decision on the future of Australia's largest gas project.

*

Amid this tedium, one small but odd division between the sides emerged. A year earlier, when Prime Minister Anthony Albanese had announced energy bill rebates, Opposition Leader Peter Dutton had criticised the policy for not being means-tested: "Frankly I think the money would be better provided to those more in need." That had an oddly Labor ring to it. The theme reappeared when Albanese, during the campaign, announced that his government would subsidise batteries for solar-powered homes and Dutton warned this was effectively forcing those who couldn't afford batteries to subsidise those who could. And again: Labor announced that its housing policy would remove a means test, opening it to everyone, while Dutton, that same day, announced a policy with an income cap.

The position of the parties had reversed. The Liberal Party was targeting those with less money: "those more in need." Labor was attempting to reach every voter.

This was in line with the way Albanese had described one mission of the Labor Party in his first press conference upon taking the leadership. The newly elected leader of his party declared, "Labor should be the natural party of government in this country." He gave a reason: "We stand for the vast majority of interests in this country."

You can make the argument: a party, once elected to government, should work to create a country which will serve most of its people. This is not quite the same, though, as saying Labor stands for "the vast majority of interests in this country." It is not that far away from saying, "We are all things to all people." Or perhaps not far enough away.

"I am a progressive," Albanese said near the beginning of that speech. He emphasised his consistency over time, as well: his approach to politics had not changed with the years. And he delivered a paragraph which, while not quite contradictory, sounded as though he were trying to have his cake and eat it too: "I do have strong values. I do have strong ideas. That doesn't mean they are not open to change because the truth is when facts change, you should change and you should always be open to engagement."

*

Two weeks before the 2022 election, in which the Australian people decided he would become their thirty-first prime minister, Albanese declared he didn't know why someone would go into politics if they didn't want to leave a legacy. He had spoken about a legacy in his first speech to parliament, he said. And he wanted to change people's lives for the better. "I want to talk about cheaper childcare. I want to talk about women's equality. I want to talk about First Nations recognition in our constitution with an enshrined Voice to Parliament."

He went on to list things he actually wanted to do. But his first words about specific legacies at this crucial political moment were about *what he wanted to talk about*. It seemed like an obvious slip: he meant these were the changes he wanted to make.

In the years that followed, it often felt as though the slip was closer to the truth. A year later, the government increased childcare subsidies; a year after that, the savings families made had been all but wiped out by inflation. Other actions were taken; there were good moves towards cheaper childcare for poorer families. Late in the term, there were rumours of a far bigger announcement on universal childcare, but it ended up delayed until the second term. It now seems possible such changes won't actually happen until the third.

And of course, "talk about" First Nations representation was all Albanese ever got to do, when the Voice proposal was soundly defeated.

*

At the 2025 election, the Albanese government became the first in this country to increase the number of seats it held at the end of its full first term. Commentators, including me, gave different reasons but agreed on one thing: Albanese must be doing something right.

*

What does it mean when we say that somebody "believes" something? Or let's start somewhere more personal. What do *you* mean when you say that you believe something?

For myself, I think it is a mix of elements, none of them particularly sharp or clear: a loosely held sense of the way things should be; some moral compass inside myself. It is probably clearest not when I am asked the direct question but when I have to react to something somebody else is saying or doing. Then I feel some movement within myself, I respond, something feels right or it feels wrong, and I can express a conviction. It is this movement within that most strongly points to my belief. I find I know what I think.

At an old pub in Sydney, talking about this essay, a friend suggests that belief is at once more deeply and more vaguely felt than we apprehend: that we should pay attention to the way it resides in memories, images, the parts of society with which you identify yourself. He is not religious but says to me that he could never be not-Catholic, nor not-Labor. This is a matter of his history, his family, the memories he has, the suburbs in which he grew up.

And now that you have thought about what you mean by "believe," I have other questions: exactly what is it that you believe? Is it something you are able to articulate? Or is the idea that you do, in fact, believe something solid merely an idea you hold about yourself, one you have held – held onto – for years without properly examining?

*

In late 2024 I was driving to get my son from his childcare centre. It was run by the Uniting Church, but this was not why he was there. It happened to be convenient, seemed welcoming and – crucially – was the only place with a free spot when we needed one. I sometimes call myself a Catholic, but my partner, whose family is very, very Catholic, makes fun of me: she says I am not really a Catholic, she likes to catch me out, not knowing little things that every true Catholic, she says, would know.

There's something in what she says. I attended a Catholic church occasionally as a child; went to a Uniting Church high school; then an Anglican college after school. I have never really belonged to a faith. This vague sense of not quite belonging has often been present in my life. We moved around a lot, and I've kept moving around a lot as an adult, so that people from Melbourne often think I'm from Sydney, while people from Sydney think I'm from Melbourne. In the Labor Party I never belonged to a faction, and people from the Left would think I was from the Right and people from the Right would assume I was from the Left. My family was neither rich nor poor. At the age of eleven I won a scholarship to a private school, which meant that I have, since then, felt comfortable with the very rich, while never feeling as though I am one of them; at the same time I don't feel I belong anywhere else, I have no historical solidarity with some other class. My parents are divorced. I am a freelance writer with no workplace. I don't feel particularly excluded and I'm far from marginalised, but I suppose that when I think about it, *belonging* is not a significant feature of my life.

In the car that day in late 2024, I thought I would call my grandfather's wife. Somehow Jo and I ended up talking about belief and she asked me what I believed. I found myself saying something about equality, and then something about the difference between equality of outcome and equality of opportunity. While there were shades of belief there, probably the strongest conclusion I took out of this conversation was that I did not know precisely how to articulate what I believed. Having worked in or around politics for twenty years and having written thousands of words on the subject, this seemed surprising, perhaps even dismaying. I felt disappointed in myself.

What has surprised me further is that, as I've talked to other people about this essay, I've found that to be quite common. Most people think they believe clear things, but then, when they are asked what those things are, soon realise it is unexpectedly hard to say.

*

The philosopher Daniel Dennett argues belief is a question of prediction. If we say somebody "believes" something, it should allow us to predict their actions. In Anil Gomes's summary: "If there is a good predictive model that works by ascribing beliefs and desires to you, then those are the beliefs and desires you really have." Gomes gives an example: "Think about the ease with which we navigate a crowded street on a rainy day. We assume that people want to avoid getting wet, and that they believe they'll get splashed if they walk too close to the kerb. That gives us a good basis for predicting the route they will take. Very often, our prediction will be correct." Dennett's argument, in other words, is that "what you believe is determined not by the goings on inside your head but by the patterns in your behaviour."

Paying close attention, then, to patterns in the behaviour of the Albanese government, we could conclude that its strongest belief is that it should talk about things.

*

And yet …

This is a little unfair, isn't it?

Examining, for the millionth time, the opening of this essay, I find myself not quite convinced. It is too harsh; perhaps, like Albanese insisting "I do have strong values. I do have strong ideas," it is working a little too hard to persuade.

The elements of the case are there: the telling phrases, the actions (or lack of action) to match. And yet I find that the story of Albanese as some kind of hollow politician, the way Scott Morrison was, does not have what Henry James described as "the blue river of truth" running through it.

While I don't want to exaggerate my knowledge, I do know Albanese; I worked with him when he was a minister. I have always respected him. In difficult situations, even when we were effectively on different sides – I worked for Julia Gillard, while he backed Kevin Rudd – I always found he had integrity. He was a man who knew his own mind and was clear about this with others.

Look at him – listen to him. He is not always compelling – but you get the sense, most of the time, that he is saying what he thinks. There is something dogged about Albanese, and you cannot be dogged unless there is something you are being dogged about; that is, unless there is somewhere to which you are doggedly heading. And it is true, too, that there is an old Labor hue to his government's concerns: wages, workers, Medicare. When he talks about leaving nobody behind, you feel he means it.

But, having tried many openings to this essay, I find the one you have just read difficult to abandon. It gets at something true. The criticisms may not be entirely fair; but nor are they entirely unfair. There is something enigmatic at the heart of this government; something that, three and a half years in, remains mysterious, opaque. The best word I have been able to come up with for this perplexing quality is "belief." What does this government believe?

*

Years ago, I proposed what a subeditor described in a headline as "Every parliament's rule of three." After a term of government, ask what three things you can recall and then decide whether you think they are good or bad. If mostly good, then you will find that the government goes on to win the next election.

As parlour games go, it's niche – but it has its use. In part, the test is a reminder that very little of what a government does is remembered. Much of governing is management. Much else is simply what any government of the time would have done. What tend to stay with us are the things that change the country: either the way we live our lives or the way our nation conceives of itself.

During the Albanese government's first term, I wrote that it was hard to think of much that would be remembered. Almost half a year into the government's second term, that hasn't changed.

This is the 100th Quarterly Essay. In the ninety-sixth, published late last year, George Megalogenis made use of my rule of three. He put it to Albanese, asking him to react to "the observation that while his government has been busy, it is risk-averse and low-key." Albanese, he wrote, "bristle[d]" at the suggestion. "He's wrong," he said. "He romanticises a mythical land that he lived in once." In other words, I was holding his government to a false standard.

Am I? Long ago, a Labor elder told me something that has remained in my mind. The mob, he said, expect "something more" from Labor – more than they expect from the Coalition.

This has become the single most important way I think about Labor: a way of considering its responsibility to the nation as well as its political appeal to voters. And yet I find myself now uncertain, wondering if it is still as true, or as important, as it once seemed. Do voters still want more from Labor? And if they do, is Labor still capable of providing it?

THE FALL

> *[Man] is a free and secure citizen of the earth, for he is attached to a chain long enough to give him access to all parts of the earth, and yet only so long that nothing can pull him over the edges of the earth. At the same time, however, he is also a free and secure citizen of heaven, for he is also attached to a heavenly chain with similar dimensions. If he wants to go to earth, the heavenly collar will choke him, if he wants to go to heaven, the earthly collar will. Yet even so, all possibilities are open to him, and he feels this; indeed, he even refuses to ascribe the whole thing to an error in the original enchainment.*
>
> Franz Kafka

Kafka was obsessed with the Fall: Adam and Eve eating of the fruit of the Tree of Knowledge. At the centre of his understanding lay two ideas. The first was that we know what is moral and what is not, but because it is so difficult to do the moral thing we spend our lives coming up with reasons for not doing it. The second was captured above: that we are always caught somewhere between heaven and earth, and that this causes us a constant agony.

*

During my time working for Kevin Rudd, boats began to arrive in what felt like large numbers. Slowly, political reality dawned: something would have to be done. I remember discussing with a foreign policy adviser the government's options – not because I had any say, but because I *wanted to know*. It quickly became apparent there were not many. I remember feeling tremendously sad. If I were a better person, this sadness would only have been for the awfulness of what would soon happen to asylum seekers. Instead, it resembled the sadness of discovering, as a child, that adults can be cruel; or perhaps, as an adult, of finding out that you have been betrayed. In those moments you learn – again – that there is no safety in this world. I would not have described myself as naive, but the naive never do. Something came home to me during that discussion, something obvious but visceral about the clash between ideals and political practice.

Not long after this, I was sorting through old clothing; a "Free the Refugees" t-shirt from university protests surfaced. My partner laughed and said, "Surely you won't be keeping that now?"

Later, years after my time as a staffer, I was approached online by an asylum seeker from Afghanistan. I was an important man, she wrote; I could speak to the minister, the prime minister. Instead, I contacted lawyers, refugee services; none was any help. The woman reached out to me again, imploring me. Again I resisted. It felt improper. It felt, too, like overstepping the bounds of my role and theirs. If I attempted to do so, the likely outcome was that they would not do anything. They would not take my calls again, either. It was not the type of thing you did. I went through other channels, followed procedure, received polite and useless letters back. One afternoon I received a call. A woman was crying, talking; I had not heard her voice before. Someone came on the line to translate; it was her son. Her family was having to split up, escape to different countries; her son had cerebral palsy; she had diabetes; something must be done. I apologised but repeated that there was nothing else I could do.

Working in politics, you become accustomed to compromise; you understand, eventually, that it is in the nature of the enterprise. But now, my time in politics long behind me, the question had been asked of me again: what did I believe? Was it what I said or what I did when push came to shove? The bleak truth was that I found, again, that what I felt and what I said had little relation to what I did. I believe I care about refugees. I have written many words criticising Australia's harsh approach. But ultimately, I have to admit that, judged by the patterns in my behaviour, I care very little about refugees.

*

Am I being too harsh on myself?

Most of the time I agree with Dennett: that behaviour is a reliable guide to what we believe. At other times, I am more forgiving – of both myself and others – and decide that our beliefs lie somewhere between what we feel and what we do. I think that all of us have beliefs, the way Kafka suggests: that we know instinctively what is to be done. And yet we live in the world. There are limits to our power. When we take account of those barriers to action, when we allow them to stop us, does that mean we no longer believe? I go back and forth on this question.

And yet: isn't this the only true test of belief? What you do when you hit what seems to be the limit of your ability to act? In Saul Bellow's novel *The Victim*, a man, Leventhal, is approached by another named Allbee. Allbee claims that in the past he was wronged by Leventhal. Now, his life a mess, he asks for Leventhal's help. Leventhal disputes the accusation, but feels a pang of obligation and offers Allbee help nonetheless. Allbee takes the help – and takes and takes. As Leventhal's own life starts to become consumed by Allbee's demands, the question is posed: at what point is Leventhal's debt paid off?

The novelist J.M. Coetzee describes the novel's "essentially religious" theme like this: "The supports for our neat, well-ordered lives can crumble at any minute; inhuman demands can without warning be made of us, and from the strangest quarters; it will be only natural to resist (Why me?); but if we want to be saved we have no choice, we must drop everything and follow."

This contrast, I think, is one that lives within Labor, or at least has and should still: the conflict between Labor's "neat, well-ordered life" – its place within Australian society, its hands on the levers of power – and the almost "inhuman demands" that it do the right thing. That is, the demand that Labor MPs be prepared to sacrifice the power they have spent their lives pursuing in order to do what they know they should.

This conflict between the purity of belief and what seems politically advisable has bedevilled centre-left parties from their beginnings. In his book *The ALP: A short history of the Australian Labor Party*, Brian McKinlay writes of the first years of Labor, before 1900:

> There was … much heart-burning on the left of the new party about the problem of advancing a socialist view of society while trying

> to keep the support of those middle-class voters who, while they might be sympathetic to the reformist aspects of Labor policy, would be likely to recoil at the suggestion of socialism. In this matter the debates within the Labor Party were a preview of what was to become a permanent and seemingly insoluble conflict – between the party's need to win office to implement reformist policies, and the strongly held belief of a section of the membership that the Labor Party should never lose sight of the socialist objective.

In 1967, Gough Whitlam addressed the Victorian branch of the ALP. He declared, "The quality of life and equality in life is what socialism is all about. In Australia, the means of raising the quality and securing equality lie in the hands of the national government." The speech, though, is most famous for his acerbic argument that Labor must, in the end, win elections: "we construct a philosophy of failure, which finds in defeat a form of justification and a proof of the purity of our principles. Certainly, the impotent are pure."

*

It would be easy to see Labor's compromises as the result of particular temporary circumstances, or as the failures of individuals. But what if failure is implicit in the mission of centre-left parties? What if there is literally no way out?

In the early years of the twentieth century, Vere Gordon Childe worked for the leader of the NSW Labor Party (before becoming a renowned archaeologist overseas). Afterwards, he wrote about what he termed the labour movement's "novel theory of democracy." This was Labor's way of ensuring MPs stayed loyal to the workers who had got them elected. The workers joined unions; the unions had a significant say over the party's policy positions; the caucus of Labor MPs was then pledged to stick to those positions; and the leader of the party was bound by the decisions of caucus. The problem is that getting elected changes people. The average MP, "surrounded by the middle-class atmosphere of Parliament," thinks more of "keeping his seat and scoring political points than of carrying out the ideal that he was sent in to give effect to." He loses touch with the workers. This process repeats for ministers, who lose touch with caucus, because they come to believe – not entirely without reason – that they have a far better understanding of the limitations they face. They also want to be re-elected.

The words of a Queensland Labor figure, Mat Reid, are worth quoting to show this problem's eternal nature and its complex psychological dimensions. He spoke in 1907:

> Opportunism will always produce Opportunists. Once you allow the politician to boss the show, he will give away everything to save himself, because he believes himself indispensable to the show, and in fact ends by becoming the show himself, and making a holy show of the rest of us. The supposed strong point made by the defaulters is their practical achievement of something in our time … legislating up to public opinion as all politicians do. But no party worthy of the name of Labour will follow public opinion; it will make and mould it.

What strikes me about this passage is that it is not only selfishness – a narrow concern with self-protection – that makes politicians betray their ideals. The justification is more complex than that: "he will give away everything to save himself, because he believes himself indispensable to the show."

*

Labor's deviation from principle is often presented as a deviation from socialism. But Labor, while deeply influenced by socialism, has never been a monolithically socialist party, which means these references to "socialism" might be more usefully understood as proxies for idealism. Labor has always been the site of a battle between purity and compromise.

Sometimes you will hear the criticism of Labor that it no longer has an ideology. But this doesn't have to be taken as criticism. Here is the great Labor speechwriter Graham Freudenberg in 1988: "There is no party in the world for which its history is of such central importance and contemporary relevance. There is a fundamental reason for this: the Australian Labor Party has never been united around an ideology."

What else, then, shapes the Labor Party? A historical loyalty to the working class, certainly. And then there is what Brian McKinlay writes of its early years: "To a degree unexpected by its founders, the new Labor Party would become a coalition of disparate elements, often linked more by hostility to the forces of Australian conservatism than by any clear bonds of common policy."

*

In the leadership challenge of early 2012, when Kevin Rudd attempted to take back his old job from Julia Gillard, Albanese declared, in tears, "I like fighting Tories. That's what I do." The phrase almost instantly became famous, both as a way of describing Albanese and as a way of expressing the passion of many Labor members.

Significantly, this phrase faces outwards, away from Labor, in keeping with McKinlay's description: a party defined by fighting its enemies.

This is echoed in Albanese's tribalism, which anyone can deduce from the list of his "three great faiths": the Labor Party, the Catholic Church and the South Sydney Rabbitohs. It is a list he returns to, again and again. Tribes are defined by boundaries; the question is not what you believe but whether you belong. And as such they are always defined as much by what they are not. Like the friend with whom I discussed belief in the pub, Albanese is telling us that he can't be not-Labor. Above all else, he is *not* a Liberal. Which more or less stands as a definition of Labor, too.

Now consider how drastically the right has changed in recent years – and how incredibly discombobulating such rapid changes must be for a party shaped around countering the right.

Remember, finally, that Labor, which for the century before Albanese's election had held power federally only about a third of the time, has *never* before been the "natural party of government" in Australia; that this is a status, a way of being, that Albanese wishes to wrest from the Liberal Party.

It is confusing to see Labor try to take on part of the Liberal Party's essence. If Labor is not *not* the Liberal Party anymore, what is it?

*

Part of the answer lies in Labor's shift, in recent years, to define itself against a new opponent. There was a time when the forces of idealism and pragmatism fought it out within the ALP. Traditionally, the Left within the ALP was the voice of idealistic opposition; this was a role Albanese played when he was younger. The Right was the voice of *whatever it takes* to win an election. Now, the Left dominates Albanese's caucus, and Albanese himself is from the Left. What happens when the Left takes power: who then provides the idealism that, as Childe warned, will always be suppressed by those in charge?

One answer – a more important answer than it may at first seem – is that this purist opposition has moved outside the party and into the Greens, via what Paul Strangio calls a "de facto split." For the Labor Party, which historically has shaped itself around not being the parties it opposes, this shift is significant. The historical confluence is crucial: just as the conservatives lose the clarity which allowed Labor to define itself against them, the Greens appear. Strangio argues that Labor "has lost an internal ginger group and a source of creative tension." I would go further still. Rather than having to accommodate that purity, find compromise with it, Labor now fights against it. "Purity" has become one definition of exactly what Labor should not be, perhaps even the most significant.

This helps make sense of one of Albanese's most important acts of self-description. Albanese describes himself as a reformist, not a revolutionary. To most, the significance will not register; it sounds like a statement of reassurance, underlining the idea Albanese will move gradually, not quickly.

In fact, it comes from a sharp historical division in the Left. I remember having this explained to me, late one night, sitting on the steps that led down to Sydney University's Students' Representative Council – which Albanese was active in decades before. The various groups always wanted to recruit people, and I was having trouble deciding which part of the left to join. Labor Left, which my girlfriend was in, was "reformist," I was told. They believed in working within the system to make changes and improve society. The Activist Left, meanwhile, was "revolutionary." Naturally, they believed a revolution was necessary – and that the "reforms" Labor pursued merely delayed that revolution and were complicit with the powerful right wing of society. Members of the Activist Left would more or less spit out the word "reformist," believing Labor a defeatist, traitorous thing to be. Those in Labor Left would spit back, "Trots," meaning Trotskyists, scorn in their voices for what they saw as futile egotism.

This is still, in essence, the division between Labor and the Greens. It always surprises outsiders just how much the two groups hate each other. In part this is because they are fighting for the same voters. Some of it is historical bad blood: Labor's anger at the Greens' behaviour, particularly during the Rudd–Gillard years.

But in part, I am certain, it is because each hates the other for being what they cannot be – for pointing to an absence in themselves. The Greens are pure, and therefore impotent. They hate Labor for its compromises, but they hate it too because it has a history of achievements that the Greens will never have. Labor people, meanwhile, hate the Greens for standing in their way, for complaining that nothing Labor does is quite good enough – but they hate the Greens too because they know there is truth in the criticisms. There is a part of Labor MPs that would like to be pure and which hates that they are not.

*

You could argue – as Albanese does, when he points out that Hawke was attacked by the left too – that we should be careful not to exaggerate the importance of the criticisms Labor faces now. It has always been attacked for being insufficiently pure; it should continue on its way and not concern itself too much with such attacks.

But perhaps the more useful way to see this struggle – between Labor's socialist objective and its reformist strategy for winning elections, between idealism on one hand and pragmatism on the other – is that it is the struggle itself that has always defined Labor. It is not that one is necessarily correct, the other misguided. Rather, it is the very existence of that struggle that keeps Labor new, that keeps it driving forward, looking for a way to knit together its desire for radical change with its reformist ambitions.

This is probably the moment at which to note how little dissent we hear from within the federal Labor Party – how rare it is to hear backbenchers saying something with which the leadership of the party might disagree. We hear barely a peep out of cabinet; and scarcely more out of all those many Labor MPs not bound by cabinet confidentiality. Albanese asserts this as a virtue, saying in September 2025 that he had never seen the party so united. "Some of the old ideological divides in the party have just disappeared … We have an ideology, but it is one in which there is a great deal of consensus across the Labor Party that people don't go into a room with the Left hat on or a Right hat on. People go in with the Labor hat."

In late August, Labor announced it would pay the government of Nauru hundreds of millions of dollars to take some asylum seekers with questions over their character. At the next caucus meeting, there were reportedly no questions on the topic. In the caucus meeting before that, there were no questions at all – about anything.

If there is still a struggle within Labor, it is going on very quietly.

Political parties prize unity. But the recent fact that Peter Dutton was often praised for his party's unity – before leading his party to historic defeat – should remind us of how hard it can be to spot the distinction between cooperation and submission; between solidarity and insipid obedience. One might easily become the other, unnoticed until it is too late; one might even be both at once.

*

The importance of this struggle is not romantic fancy; it has been borne out by history. The philosopher Richard Rorty has written about the division in the American left, between old-school reformers and the New Left who preached revolution. He places himself on the side of the reformers and defends their accomplishments. But he also credits the rage and impatience of the 1960s New Left, their demands for revolution, with driving change that would otherwise not have been possible: both civil rights and an end to the Vietnam War. "Their loss of patience was the result of perfectly justified, wholly sincere moral indignation – moral indignation which, the New Left rightly sensed, we reformists were too tired and too battered to feel."

It was true in the United Kingdom as well. John McTernan, who advised both Tony Blair and Julia Gillard (and was a colleague of mine), recently wrote:

> A plane, as the saying goes, needs two wings – so do parties of the centre Left. The intellectual energy and the idealism of the broader Left have always been central. Every successful Labour government – and every Labour landslide – has drawn from its Left.
>
> In 1945 for Attlee it was nationalisation and the National Health Service. In the sixties for Wilson it was sex and race equality and social reforms like divorce, abortion and the legalisation of homosexuality. In 1997, Tony Blair and New Labour drew strongly on the social, cultural and political analysis of [the journal] *Marxism Today* and delivered a massive expansion of rights to workers, increased income for lower paid workers through tax credits and the minimum wage, and constitutional reform including devolution.

*

My feeling is that this struggle is important for another reason, too. I think there is something in it that speaks to all of us; something that has traditionally made centre-left parties capable of speaking to great numbers of people. This is because that struggle is in all of us. This is what Kafka saw. It is true there is a *right* thing to do. But it is also true that we are defined by the struggle to choose between what is right and what we judge can be done, and by the struggle to tell the difference between the two. It is the nature of being a human in the world.

There is, of course, no way of conceiving of what it might be to pursue ideals unencumbered by the world. Whitlam was not quite right when he said "the impotent are pure," because they, too, are choosing within this world. When they fail, they fail absolutely, with nothing to show for it, a failure potentially even more devastating than compromised success. This is, in essence, the philosophy that drives Labor: there is no such thing as purity. It is a legitimate argument.

But there can be no failure unless there is some aim in mind; otherwise, what is failure to be judged against? What "the impotent" had over modern iterations of Labor is that, when they failed, they knew it. It was an honest failure.

This was the importance of that socialist objective for Labor; and of the idea that Labor represented the working class. When a Labor government compromised, it was compromising something; when it betrayed the working class, there was somebody specific it betrayed. What ideal does Labor have now? As historian Stuart Macintyre put it thirty years ago, "True believers need beliefs."

The point is not that Labor should sincerely pursue its socialist objective. It is that without some articulated ideal, the only measure against which you can be judged becomes time in office: how many elections did you win? You can then point at what was done and say, "There – we achieved exactly what was possible."

There may be a distinction between Labor's current approach and the old Labor Right approach of "whatever it takes," but it is not easy to say what it is.

Does Labor still know what should be done? What ideal still attracts Labor, exerting an equal and opposite force to the earthly, practical desire for political power, refreshing the struggle that must always be there if the party is to live: not just survive, but live?

When I was twenty, Bill Clinton and Tony Blair were leaders of their countries. In Australia, we had John Howard. I saw hope in those two men; in what seemed to be the exciting new left-wing movement they were creating. Even now, it is easy for me to slip back into thinking of them as revolutionaries of sorts: the progenitors of a new era. And I think that is understandable, given the usual desire of progressive parties to change the world. "New Labour" captured an atmosphere and was an effective piece of propaganda, sounding like it should be both those things: *new* and *Labour*.

In fact – and I am far from the first to note this – it was neither. The historian Gary Gerstle gives Blair and Clinton their true historical significance: as the leaders who acquiesced in the political order crafted by their conservative predecessors. Gerstle suggests that history is best understood as a series of political or economic orders. An order is "a constellation of ideologies, policies, and constituencies that shape … politics in ways that endure beyond the two-, four-, and six-year election cycles." The true test of an order, Gerstle writes, "is when the opposition acquiesces to an order's ideological and policy imperatives." The Republican president Dwight Eisenhower acquiesced in Franklin Roosevelt's New Deal order. In the 1990s, Clinton and Blair became the left-wing Eisenhowers: the leaders who acquiesced in the order imposed by Ronald Reagan and Margaret Thatcher. Gerstle follows many others in calling this order "neoliberal."

*

It is easy to get bogged down defining neoliberalism. I like Perry Anderson's summary: "the most radical expression and theorization" of capitalism. My own sense is that it is two things. First, a system geared towards widening the gap between rich and poor by a relentless focus on individualism, privatisation, deregulation and markets. Second, the sense we all have that money and economics are our contemporary gods. It is, in short, the world we now live in; the one we think of as normal.

Neoliberalism is what Margaret Thatcher was talking about when she once said, "There is no alternative." After the death of the socialist experiment, as the Berlin Wall fell and the Soviet Union dissolved, Thatcher's assertion turned prophetic: there literally was no alternative.

This was a massive shift for the centre-left. Socialism had given it a purpose of sorts, even if not always taken literally; an ideal pulling parties of the centre-left towards it. Then it died. Meanwhile, just as the left was being rendered directionless, the right was gaining momentum from precisely the same events.

This was true not only of the right's morale, its gathering sense that it had been correct all along and now had the proof. It was also true of the way power shifted. Gerstle suggests that the fear of communism's spread had previously encouraged the forces of capital to compromise with workers. Big business could not risk pushing unions too far – what if communism was the result? – and so gave in to a reasonable number of demands. After 1991, Gerstle writes, "the pressure on capitalist elites and their supporters to compromise with the working class vanished."

Wages began to fall. As capitalism spread across the world, more markets opened up. If workers in America pushed back too hard, businesses could hire workers elsewhere. The right, along with the forces of capital, became stronger. The left weakened.

*

One way to distinguish a political order from a passing fad, Gerstle argues, is that it carries with it "a moral perspective able to inspire voters with visions of the good life." He has pointed to Reagan's use of "freedom," meaning both economic freedom and individual freedom. After Reagan comes Bill Clinton, who sees a world coloured by this freedom: to travel, to partake of other cultures, to pursue personal adventure.

We have here a "good life" that traverses left and right, that takes in elements of each and becomes a kind of idealised life that reflects the dominant political order. It's not quite right to say the political order *produces* that vision of the good life; rather, they reinforce each other. They are intertwined and rise together.

Slowly, though, this "good life" entwined with the neoliberal economic order began to appear unattainable. You could still travel overseas, sample cuisines, be whoever you wanted to be. But three things shifted. The first was a growing sense that these delights were not available to everyone; that there would always be a chasm between those who could benefit from them and those who could not. Second, for many of those who could, there was still a trade-off. You could have those things, but not a house; you could not count on a secure job. The third element affected everyone. Even if you could somehow avoid those trade-offs, there was a growing sense that something else was missing. Something that gave life a certain texture.

Is it possible to say what changed? One thing: our experience of time. We are always busy now. Being productive feels like a moral imperative. Another: we are always on our screens. This is the dominant fact of our time, one we have only just begun to grasp – the way screens separate us from the world, from each other, from ourselves. I am always interrupting conversations with the people I love to hear news or jokes from people I don't know; to read a message from an acquaintance. These interruptions pile up until they are a significant portion of my life.

More and more, it feels like this supposed good life is not in fact a good life.

*

Should I bother to connect this hunch to facts? Does anyone seriously doubt that there is something broken in our society?

One of Labor's frontbenchers, Andrew Leigh, told *Guardian Australia* that "we're now as unequal as the US was in 1980 … Track that [trend] through another generation and suddenly … things start to look much, much more like US-style inequality." As the *Guardian* put it, Australia is just one generation away from looking like the United States with regard to wealth distribution. And we all know what is happening there right now.

The ABC reported that on school performance, Australia has been getting worse for twenty years, with one expert saying we "had the steepest and most consistent decline in achievement in the entire world." In the world!

A fact I find more disturbing still: the "learning gap" between kids from advantaged and disadvantaged backgrounds does not shrink during school – it widens. Our school system is making inequality worse. Everybody knows that Medicare bulk billing is not what it was; our health system does not feel free or universal in the way it once did. Our universities are dying. A huge proportion of students are from overseas, which is an indication of the universities' focus: making money. Efficiency, profit and marketing have taken over from education and edification as the central tasks of our institutions of higher learning.

Increasingly, Australians do not believe they can earn enough in their own right ever to buy a home. Increasingly, they are correct. If your parents aren't wealthy, your chances of owning property are declining. And it is not just housing. Baby boomers – not uniformly, but overall – are becoming wealthier still, as investment values soar. Meanwhile, more young adults than ever before are dependent on their families to help them with living expenses.

It is not, then, just a vibe, the curmudgeon's belief that things are only ever getting worse. Our society is changing; it has been changing for some time. The suspicion many of us have that there is something troubling about the way we live finds its correlative in the material facts of life in this country.

*

This diminution of what we can expect from life has been occurring at exactly the same time as we have become convinced no other life is possible.

A sharp division between existence fifty years ago and now is that many people were able to articulate what they believed with a word or two. They might have said, "I'm a communist" or "I'm an anti-communist." Some would have said, "I'm a socialist." Others might have said they were democratic socialists; or perhaps social democrats. Such labels were crucial to many people's sense of themselves. We think now of McCarthyism mostly in terms of an illiberal society cracking down on those who wouldn't toe the line. But it is also true that McCarthyism points us to how strongly held such beliefs were: it was a time when people saw their careers destroyed for holding the belief that there was a better social and economic system.

People are still penalised for belief today; in some ways we are in a new McCarthyist moment. But penalising people for beliefs about different economic systems now would seem ridiculous, not because we are more enlightened, but because these types of beliefs have been rendered harmless. As experiments in these different types of societies failed and made clear the immense human costs they had exacted, the landscape of belief flattened out. No longer was there a mountain range: there was simply a vast plain, labelled "capitalism." Rather than each of us living around one of those mountains, we were scattered chaotically across this landscape. Some of us might believe in stronger social safety nets; some of us leaned more towards letting the market rip. But nobody was against markets; nobody wanted to tear up the social safety net entirely. We were now differentiated along the lines of specific policies: perhaps we believed there should be choice in schools, or healthcare, or not. Decades later, the range of beliefs it is common to hold has constricted further, as the society in which we live has become taken for granted. Nobody really seriously proposes knocking down the private schools. We might think they should not get government funding – but even this sounds a little extreme, and most people who think this way would likely suggest instead, publicly at least, that their access to funding be slowly restricted, over decades.

A belief like this is important. Schools policy is important! But it is important to recognise how little we are now willing to countenance as genuine options for change; how incredibly limited the range of beliefs it now seems permissible to have.

*

This change affects us all; it is why so many of us find it difficult to say what we believe. But it is a particular problem for the left, which has lost an important way of describing – both to others and itself – what it aims to do.

The American philosopher Susan Neiman writes, "It's not accidental that most of those who would have called themselves leftists a generation ago now call themselves progressives. Fear is a factor. In a world where residues of the Cold War have yet to be examined, much less discarded, 'leftist' sounds too close to 'socialist,' and 'socialist' too close to the state socialism of Eastern Europe for comfort."

Albanese describes himself today as "progressive." In his maiden speech to parliament, though, twenty-nine years ago, Albanese described himself as a "democratic socialist." Early this year, Albanese was asked by *The Squiz*'s Kate Watson what this meant. Albanese said:

> What it means to be a member of the Labor Party, something I was drawn to, I say that I was raised with three great faiths, the Labor Party, the Catholic Church and South Sydney Rugby League Football Club, by my mum. And that represents, I guess, on the left–right spectrum, some of it is a bit of nonsense, but it means, in general, that your starting point is you recognise that society is more than just individuals, that there is collective responsibility, if you like. And so that is a bit of a starting point, that you think that society is also judged by how it looks after the most vulnerable and provides that opportunity, and that government has a role in that. If you put the sort of, at an extreme, on the left spectrum, government has a role to look after people, on the right spectrum, if government just gets out of the way and disappears, then people will be better off. Now, I tend towards government does have a role in looking after people and in looking after shaping the economy as well where market failure occurs.

Note that Albanese doesn't quite address the question about democratic socialism; he seems to swerve, to define instead "what it means to be a member of the Labor Party." He is cautious, too, when talking about the left of the political spectrum. At "an extreme," he says, "government has a role to look after people" – which is hardly an extreme position, even for conservatives. Finally, note how mediated is his description of his own beliefs. He merely "tend[s] towards" the view that "government does have a role in looking after people" and "in shaping the economy as well where market failure occurs." "A role" is, again, an uncontroversial position for almost anyone in politics.

Perhaps I am being too generous – relying on my personal knowledge of Albanese – but when I read this my first thought is not that Albanese does not believe things. It is, instead, that he sounds reluctant to give voice to what he believes. He sounds oddly sheepish, almost apologetic: "some of it is a bit of nonsense."

But this is only a hunch. The difficulty is that, in practice, there is no real way of distinguishing between a politician who won't say what he believes and one who doesn't know.

I think back to the words used by Rorty and McTernan, the elements of the broader left that Labor must find a way to include within itself. *Intellectual energy. Idealism. Rage. Impatience.* They are not words you would associate with many centre-left parties today. What is Labor angry about? What is it impatient to fix?

Poverty? Three-quarters of a million Australian children live in poverty. Last year, the advocate Toni Wren told me the government was ignoring child poverty, that it wouldn't even name the problem. I said she sounded more frustrated than she had before, to which she said, "They've had two more years." A year later, little has changed.

Or take one of Labor's proudest acts: delivering public schools the funding promised under the Gonski reforms. By this, it means the full funding will be delivered by 2034 – which means there are children starting school this year who will not get the funding they need until their schooling is almost over.

One of the reasons I struggle with my opinion of this government – why I constantly second-guess myself – is that it is so much a matter of seeing what is not there. There is no long list of egregious actions. Instead, there are absences. And sometimes even the absences are unclear – something is being done, but so slowly it is hard to be sure any difference is being made. Constantly, it seems, Labor is doing enough to raise the suspicion that belief is involved in what it does, but not enough to put the matter to rest.

*

In 2023 the prime minister told right-wing commentator Piers Morgan that he was "a social democrat who believes in markets, but believes that the state, the power of the state, can make a positive difference to people's lives." This is so old hat now as to be unremarked, but really its dreadful blandness should shock us: the fact that much of the social-democratic left feels it can or should define its political position as "believing in markets." It is a way, of course, to run away from socialism; to avoid the accusation of being a socialist. Which means that it is really a way of disavowing strong belief, not a way of claiming it.

Earlier this year, Jim Chalmers described the government as "centrist." I put this same label to Albanese in 2023. He replied, "I think we're Labor." This is similar to his description of the way factions had shed old ideological divides: "People go in with the Labor hat."

What is Labor's vision of the good life? Or, alternatively, what is its view of the life we are leading now: with our broken education system, our broken housing system, our deteriorating health system, our rising inequality? Topic by topic, Labor declares it wants to fix these problems. But problems like these do not exist in isolation. They are built on a foundation of assumptions: about what is acceptable and what is not; about what is set in stone and what might still be changed; about the way things work. On the broader question of the society in which they all exist and are related, we do not hear much.

*

I think Neiman is wrong to say such swerves away from explicit statement of belief are driven by fear. Once, definitely. Today, with the Cold War a distant memory (and not even a memory for many), it feels more like embarrassment.

Embarrassment is always lurking, when it comes to belief. On one hand, we think we *should* have beliefs. To accuse somebody of believing nothing is one of the worst things it is possible to say about a person. And yet when others tell us of their beliefs, we find it hard to take them entirely seriously. We inevitably find the convictions of others a little too pompous, a little too sincerely held – which is why, when we say someone is "very earnest," we never quite mean it as a compliment.

It is possible that the centre-left has gone for so long without saying what it believes that it has forgotten. Or perhaps it knows, but, anticipating the shaming, mocking reaction of others – the bullying of the Murdoch press and the conservative parties – finds itself unwilling to declare it. It is not so long ago that Kevin Rudd was mercilessly ridiculed for declaring climate change the greatest moral challenge of our time – despite (or perhaps because of) the fact that he was right.

Articulating a belief is, after all, a little like blowing out candles and then telling someone what we have just wished – because isn't belief a wish of sorts, a desire for the world to be a certain way? We do not say wishes out loud, hoping this will make them come true. But we stay silent for another reason too: because we would be embarrassed by admitting what we really want.

For blowing out candles, this is fine. Otherwise, it is childish: as Neiman writes, the "fear of embarrassment should itself be embarrassing, the sort of thing that … ought to be left behind when you're grown." Parties of the centre-left need to find a way to articulate what they want. Those wishes may not come true. But it may be that politics works the opposite way to blowing out candles: that saying something out loud is the only hope you have of making something come about.

During the 2022 election campaign, the wife of a friend sewed a banner. Later, she presented it to her local MP, who presented it to Albanese. Across it ran a single word: "Absolutely." That was Albanese's answer, in the final fortnight of that campaign, to a question about whether he would support the minimum wage being raised by 5.1 per cent. It exploded from the banal mass of campaign-speak: a clear, decisive declaration of belief.

After the election, the Fair Work Commission delivered the pay rise. In fact, Albanese's success in driving up wages is perhaps the most significant achievement of his first term, one brought about by working doggedly at different policy areas. Submissions were made to the Fair Work Commission. Workers in aged care and childcare – often poorly paid, mostly female – were supported. Unions were given expanded rights to bargain. The government approached inflation with one eye on prices and the other on jobs and wages, standing up to critics who wanted more austerity sooner.

We don't treat the making of election promises as a remarkable thing, but perhaps we should. Promises, in themselves, are remarkable: philosophers recognise them as a very particular type of speech act. They are not just speech but a form of action too: as the philosopher John Searle put it, a promise "is, by definition, an act of placing oneself under an obligation." You might still break your promise; but you have, nonetheless, increased the likelihood that you will do the thing you've pledged to do. To cast back to Dennett's definition of belief, it makes it more likely you will create a pattern of behaviour that makes your beliefs clear.

Albanese places great store in keeping promises. A year into government, journalist David Crowe interviewed him.

> So what does he say to those who voted for him a year ago but hoped for bigger targets on climate change, a more generous increase in unemployment benefits or a stronger helping hand for single mothers?

> "What isn't the right thing to do is to put forward positions that can't be delivered," he says. "That leads to disillusionment and undermines the integrity of what you're putting forward."

There is some truth to this. But it ignores the fact that making a promise can itself be a useful thing to do, much like setting a deadline: it compels you to achieve something you otherwise might not.

This is true even if you don't quite reach your goal. During another election campaign, in 1987, Bob Hawke made a pledge: that by 1990 no Australian child would be living in poverty. At the same time, he announced a new payment to help reach that goal. Hawke never achieved what he said he would. But his actions – tied to his words – still brought about a significant achievement: reducing child poverty by a third.

We have here an illustration of the relationship between words and actions and belief. The words you use make your actions more likely; your actions then give your words meaning, making them more than "just words." The belief, then, emerges from both. In one sense, you can understand Albanese's reluctance to over-promise; he says that he would much rather over-deliver. But you can also observe in this a more specific version of the centre-left's embarrassment about talking of the society it wants to build. Here, we see a reluctance even to talk openly of the steps Labor wants to take along the way.

Saying something out loud is not only brave; it can be a way of making yourself brave. Or to put this another way: if you can't even bring yourself to say what you want to do, what chance is there you will actually do it? An earlier draft of Hawke's speech read, "No child need live in poverty." Graham Freudenberg, who wrote the line for Hawke, changed it in later versions, dismissing the "bureaucratic caution" which gave Hawke a loophole. The language Freudenberg gave to Hawke was braver – and brave acts are built on brave language.

Passive language, then, might well make you passive: in which case we should pay attention to Albanese's language, which seems to write him out of the picture. Take his phrasing above: his desire not to "put forward positions that can't be delivered." "Can't be delivered" by the government, he means – which is in part a choice, one made by the prime minister, not an objective fact.

Albanese used a similar locution this September when he announced an emissions reduction target. He justified the target – which is unlikely to be enough to help keep temperature rises below 1.5°C – partly by asserting it was "achievable." But that word has no clear meaning, because what the government decides it wants to achieve has a significant bearing on what ends up becoming achievable. Like saying "We're Labor," it is circular – and leaves you similarly confused about what this government actually wants to do.

*

Hawke's pledge on child poverty had another effect, too. Freudenberg believed it played a significant part in Labor's victory that year. "One had to be in the Sydney Opera House to grasp the transformative effect of this promise. There was still life in the old Labor Party and it galvanised the whole campaign for a hard-won victory."

Part of the appeal of promises is the risk at which they put the promiser. If I promise something easy – that I will go to sleep tonight – well, who cares? But promising something that might not be delivered is to go out on a limb; to place myself in peril of a sort. Hawke was not only promising something noble, but also something extraordinarily difficult. There is – much like the struggle between purity and pragmatism – something human in this. By placing your own integrity on the line, you are giving tangible form to the fact you care about this thing.

Strangely enough, this applies also to broken promises. Perhaps the most electrifying moment of Albanese's prime ministership, so far, came when he decided to break his promise on the stage-three tax cuts. This time, Albanese was not keeping his word. But it was electrifying because Albanese was still risking something – himself.

Yet even in this moment, the prime minister seemed unwilling to make much of a Labor argument for the changes. Instead, as the historian Frank

Bongiorno has noted, he repeatedly leaned on the fact they went to every single taxpayer, "right up and down the income ladder." Jim Chalmers told reporters, "This is about one thing and one thing only – more help with the cost of living for more Australians." The wealthy had the size of their tax cut significantly reduced – but it remained pretty big. If you earned $200,000 a year, under the previous arrangement you received a $9000 tax cut; under Labor's changes, you still kept half.

*

These two exciting Albanese moments stand out because there have been so few during his time as leader. One of them, remember, occurred before he was prime minister. To the broken promise, you could add Albanese's declaration that he would pursue an Indigenous Voice to Parliament. You can argue – as many have – that pursuing it was unwise, but it was also a promise kept, a noble cause and a courageous choice.

Otherwise, the government has been marked by a strong aversion to risk. Some of this was the result of the referendum loss; and some, quite reasonably, was because of the great difficulty in pursuing anything other than cost-of-living fixes in a period of high inflation.

But the tendency was there from the start, perhaps stemming from Labor's small initial majority. Privately, even in its first year, Labor would talk about not frightening the horses, regarding this as an achievement. Its policies often seemed finely calibrated to avoid creating opponents – something was done, but not so much that anybody might get upset.

Labor increased the tax paid by large gas companies, but kept the hike small enough that they did not even complain (understandably – their share prices rose when the tiny increase was announced). New rules were introduced for competition between supermarkets, but the government promised it would not break them up. It would do something about gambling ads, just not the ban that had been called for. It would do its best to stop bank scams, but would not force banks to reimburse customers – which meant banks had limited incentive to improve protections.

Again and again the government seeks the path of least resistance. Sometimes this means abandoning policies about which you think Labor might be more resolute. Before the 2022 election, Labor promised it would stop religious schools discriminating against LGBTQIA+ students and teachers. In government, though, it said it would not proceed without bipartisan support – which, predictably, it didn't get. Labor walked away.

Or consider once more – because it is, after all, Australia's intended contribution to fighting the greatest existential threat humanity faces – Albanese's announcement of his emissions reduction target, just two months ago: "we think we've got the sweet spot. There will be criticism from some who say it's too high, there's some who will say that it's too low." This was not all Albanese meant by "sweet spot" – he meant, too, that the targets did something useful scientifically without damaging the country economically. But you don't have to be glib about it to recognise that there is an identification, at either a conscious or an unconscious level – probably both – of "sweet spot" and landing right in the middle of opinion.

The perfection of this approach came in the lead-up to the government's productivity summit. Early on, Jim Chalmers declared he was ready to "grasp the nettle" on tax reform. But as the summit approached, the government began talking down the idea of much coming directly out of it, certainly on tax.

The aim of the summit seemed to be to reach consensus. Albanese told *The Australian*, "If you had a choice between, do you have less things with more support, or more things with less broad support, then I'm in favour of the former."

Consensus can be useful – but that is a genuinely striking statement, for the way it privileges the level of support for an idea over the quality of an idea or the importance of the problem being solved.

*

Where is Labor's belief in all this? If you tried – on the basis of these statements and their accompanying actions – to deduce what the government believed, what would you conclude? I am reminded of a sentence from Paul Keating's speechwriter Don Watson, written when Howard was prime minister and Labor was in Opposition: "They seem to think only what they think the people think." How else to make sense of Chalmers' repeated descriptions of the government as "middle of the road"? What other way is there to take Albanese's claim that Labor represents the "vast majority of interests"?

In part, this is the result of a brutal electoral logic. Labor is sometimes accused of abandoning the working class, its original voting base and the cause which gave it purpose. This may be partially true, but it is also the case that the working class has changed; it is less monolithic, more dispersed, less unionised. Even if Labor wanted to – if it suddenly decided tomorrow that this would be its mission – there is no "working class" to which the party might return. This leaves Labor adrift, unsure who it represents, left standing for the "majority of interests."

This is just one aspect of a broader fracturing of identity in our society. It was not so long ago that many people, perhaps most, thought of themselves as "Labor people" or "Liberal people." Twenty years ago John Howard talked about this shift: in the 1960s, he said, 40 per cent reliably voted Labor, 40 per cent Liberal, with 20 per cent in the centre. The proportion of swing voters, he said, had doubled since then.

Today, the middle has grown further. At each election, a third of voters don't even give their first vote to Labor and Liberal; presumably the number that don't do so reliably is greater still. And this is part of a broader trend that has been developing for decades, most famously outlined in Robert D. Putnam's book *Bowling Alone*. Once, people divided themselves up by their identities, tied to institutions, which were tied to beliefs. In Australia, people were mostly Catholics or Protestants. Perhaps they belonged to Rotary or the Lions. Those religious faiths had ties to the major parties. And these beliefs, identities and institutions were bound up in another form of meaning, which was community. That might sound like a vague concept, except that it did not only exist in some intangible sense but in the form of actual groups which met regularly: church groups, sporting clubs, party branches.

In recent decades, all this has broken down. To win over the growing numbers of uncommitted voters, political parties have developed two campaign strategies. Frank Bongiorno describes one approach:

> Political scientists developed the idea of the "catch-all party," which collects the support of various classes, cohorts and demographics in its endeavour to get a majority. The parties can only succeed in this endeavour by offering policies that often look disconnected and lacking in "narrative" because each is calculated to appeal to a specific set of voters.

This is what we saw in the lead-up to the 2025 election, as Labor crafted policies to win the votes of particular groups: debt forgiveness for students, deposit help for first homebuyers. Neither addressed fundamental problems – university fees remained exorbitant and poorly designed, while the housing policy would in fact push up prices – but then that wasn't the point.

The second approach is to offer policies which appeal to the broadest possible group – what used to be called the lowest common denominator.

Together, these result in a politics of the bland. The first does so by creating a thousand tiny policies, largely forgettable. The second discards anything that might offend.

*

What has happened to advocacy – to the belief that a central task of politics is changing people's minds? Approaching the productivity summit, Chalmers said that if it failed, "It won't be a shortage of courage, but a shortage of consensus." This was a nice-sounding bit of nonsense: if there were consensus, then no courage from the government would be required.

In a 1990 phone call with journalist Laurie Oakes, Paul Keating said, "I'm in the crazy-brave category … You've got to stand for what you believe." He told Oakes that inflation had to be broken, and that you couldn't do it by gingerly sidestepping a recession. "I'm prepared to chance my hand and take the whole show to the wire." Five years earlier he had made the case for a goods and services tax at a summit Hawke had called. Very publicly, Keating lost. Here is what he had to say about it:

> I fought it out in the country and in front of the public under the cameras in a tax summit. I do not mind taking the losses. If the judgment is we cannot introduce a broadly-based consumption tax, that there is not enough public support and that the inflationary influences of its introduction were too much for the country and the fabric of the economy to stand, I accept that judgment; but the fact is I tried …

Keating did, ultimately, concede, including to public opinion – but not before chancing his arm. We have here again the risk that excites – and that Albanese took on with tax cuts and the Voice. One success and one failure. And yet you get the impression that Labor is absolutely terrified of repeating its failure; and not sufficiently emboldened by its one successful fight to attempt such a thing again. It has not yet accepted – as any good government must – that failure is the price you must pay, more often than you would like, for pursuing your convictions.

Keating used to say he was in the "conflict business." Years after politics he put it still more bluntly: "I'm not in the consensus business … Fuck consensus. I'm in the conflict business." When he was still prime minister, he would invite ministers back to the Lodge to listen to Mahler, as a way of reminding them that, in the end, what they were doing amounted to "dust between the floorboards." Therefore, he said, "Why would we take second quality decisions? Why wouldn't we do better?"

The two positions are connected. If you want the very best outcome – not simply the one which you can convince most people to support – then conflict is inevitable. You may not win, but that is not the same as deciding not to fight.

*

There is another problem with the market-based approach to politics, the desire to give the people only what you think they want. This problem stems from the way that capitalism, in the form in which it exists now – that is, neoliberalism – seems to us the only possible system; that, in the words of theorist Mark Fisher, "it is now impossible even to *imagine* a coherent alternative to it."

It is plausible – perhaps even likely, given the steady drop in the share of the vote going to the major parties – that many of us want something different from what we have. That is, more dramatic transformation than just a series of small improvements to existing mechanisms, step changes to the way things are already done. But it also seems as though we have stopped believing that such change is possible.

This isn't about scrapping the system and starting again – some stubborn or forlorn utopianism. It is more localised than that. Can any of us imagine, anymore, really, a society in which we did not have what amounts to segregation in our schooling system, between rich and poor? In which private health funds, which we are penalised for not joining, did not rip us off? In which the things that matter most in our lives – childcare, healthcare, aged care, schooling – were not damaged and degraded by the profit motive, cost reductions, higher fees?

What if we have all stopped being able to conceive of what we want – not because we don't want it, but because our imaginations have become limited, our language stunted? In this scenario, political parties might look like they were delivering what people want; they might even harvest a significant number of votes. But people's unhappiness would continue rising. Their deepest desires would remain unfulfilled. Centre-left parties – those which traditionally traffic in hope – would appear oddly listless. And faith in our democracy, its institutions and its actors would continue falling.

One might think, in such a scenario, that it might fall to a party like Labor to do at least some of the imagining for the rest of us. It might even discover some political opportunity in this.

*

On occasion, you get a hint of the government's willingness to resist the neoliberal mindset. One surprising achievement of the Albanese government is its restrictions on social media for children under sixteen. It was a clear decision; not an easy one; and, crucially, one founded on a moral viewpoint.

Many on the left expressed outrage; many landed on the impossibility of delivering the change, an oddly technocratic objection. As social psychologist Jonathan Haidt has pointed out, legislating creates an incentive. After all, he says, social media companies figured out how to hold auctions for online ads involving thousands of companies in the time it takes to load a webpage. "This is a miracle of technical innovation. And they did that because there was money in it. And now the question is: Do you think maybe they could figure out if somebody is under sixteen or over sixteen?"

In other words, here was a Labor leader refusing to take the objections of multi-billion-dollar corporations seriously and instead using the power of government to get businesses to do what they always say they are good at – innovating – in the name of something he judged important.

You can have rational discussions about the pros and cons of screen time. In the end, though, as the political writer Ezra Klein has said, there does not have to be a utilitarian reason. It is possible to say, "It's just bad. I just don't want you looking at the screen all the time. I think it's not the way to be a human being."

The reason Albanese's intervention here is worth noting is this last point: it relates to the question that is always at the centre of politics, how to be a human being. Labor made a similar move by legislating for the "right to disconnect": if you are at home, you do not have to be contactable by your boss. Both of these interventions are tied to visions of a good life – one that is significantly different from the "good life" to which neoliberalism has accustomed us.

In Albanese's election-night speech in May 2025, he said:

> Today, the Australian people have voted for Australian values. For fairness, aspiration and opportunity for all. For the strength to show

> courage in adversity and kindness to those in need … Australians have chosen to face global challenges, the Australian way – looking after each other, while building for the future.

Amid the things any politician might say – "aspiration" and "courage in adversity" – there are some clear, compelling phrases that seem personal for Albanese: *Looking after each other. Kindness to those in need.* These are calls to conscience – demands for action similar to the "essentially religious" demand Coetzee described, to "drop everything and follow."

I had a similar reaction – a recognition of morality in the midst of politics – when I heard Jim Chalmers defending Labor's increase to JobSeeker payments in its first year. What worried the carping Coalition spokesperson, he said, "was that it meant that the broader Australian community would be funding help for the most vulnerable. That is the whole basis of social security." For this clear line he received applause. It was a sharp argument. But the truth is that Labor's increase to JobSeeker was fairly small, and only came in the face of sustained pressure. There has not been an increase to the rate since – outside mandated indexation – and those on JobSeeker still live in poverty.

Just occasionally, you have the sense that this Labor government knows what it wants to do. Or rather that, as Kafka suggests is true of all of us, it knows instinctively what it should be doing.

I remember my father leaving. He walked purposefully, hurriedly through the house, he was carrying bags. My mother was crying and he walked down the side of the house and away.

I remember it being a shock. Other than that, I can't remember what I felt. But after it happened I didn't tell anyone. I didn't tell my friends, not even my best friend, not for a year, and even then he found out some other way. He was furious with me. But I was deeply ashamed and could not have imagined telling anyone.

Why? Part of this was the time. Divorce was not so common – or, rather, it did not feel like it was. There was still a furtiveness about it. But alongside this sense of shame, which I am sure many children felt, lay a feeling I have already mentioned, of not belonging. It was not that I had an unhappy time at school; I had good friends, I did well, I would even say that I was happy. But I was there on a scholarship, and I was always aware that the boys around me came from richer families. They had large, beautiful houses, they took holidays to the same spots on the coast, ate at famous restaurants. There was something impermeably secure about their lives.

I observed, with greedy fascination, their attitudes to money. I remember one boy being careful with what he spent at recess, even though he lived in a fancy house – his father was a barrister, they were rich – and I remember thinking, ah, this isn't something rich people do because they're rich, this is *why* they're rich, they manage money differently. This isn't true, of course. Rich people are as varied in their habits with money as anyone else; the idea they are cleverly frugal is self-serving mythology that feeds the idea that they deserve what they have. But while I know this, there is another part of me that still believes that old tale, just as there is a part of me who is still that boy who does not have as much money as those around him.

But because I went to that school, I have never felt entirely out of place with the rich. Instead, I can mix with them; I can mimic their manners, more or less, behave in the right ways, correctly make – or refrain from making – references. But the most interesting (and perhaps damning) thing is that I am proud of this. I am proud of my ability to *pass*. Why?

Writing this now helps me make sense of my coming to work for the Labor Party. This desire to *pass*, as it turns out, has long been a part of Labor culture – and of labour parties around the world. The UK's Labour Party first held government in 1924. Political historian Malcolm Petrie, reviewing books dealing with that first effort, writes: "Labour entered office determined to disprove accusations of extremism and to show that it was a respectable party." This was, in part, about rejecting

> the accusation, voiced most bluntly by Winston Churchill in 1920 when he was still a Liberal, that Labour wasn't fit to govern. This explains the composition of the cabinet, and Labour ministers' willingness to appear in court dress, despite the unease this provoked on the political left. It is also the reason some of the party's most prominent policies were discarded as soon as it became clear that Labour could form a government. The proposed wealth tax, the capital levy, was dumped: [Chancellor of the Exchequer Philip] Snowden called it "an electoral millstone."

That Labour abandoned policies that made it seem more radical than it wished to appear sounds familiar. But this was not only about electoral success. Its members went further, even dressing the part of more "respectable" MPs. There is something psychological and emotional going on here: a deep-seated concern about inferiority, coupled with a defensive determination to prove doubters wrong. But at the same time these men were confident enough in their abilities to win government, and then to govern, if only briefly. As so often, shame and pride are two sides of the same coin, constantly spinning, showing this face, then that.

Forty years ago, in a foreword to a history of the Labor Party, then NSW premier Neville Wran pointed to a strange contradiction. The ALP, he wrote, is one of the oldest political parties in the world; it has governed often, including in crisis, and has many achievements.

> Yet – and this is the great paradox – this tremendous Australian institution, one of our few authentically Australian institutions, is still deemed in certain circles (some extremely powerful) to be on trial, as it were, as to its loyalty.
>
> There can be no complete explanation of the destruction of the Whitlam government in 1975 without reference to this enduring paradox and its powerful effect on Australian political life for at least sixty-five years. Its baleful influence cannot be discounted in any account of the destruction of the Scullin and Chifley governments, the premature death of Curtin or the undermining of the leadership of Evatt and Calwell.

Wran's point comes down to a question of legitimacy: that in some way Labor, whenever it governs, is perceived by many as an interloper.

If that sounds like ancient history, consider the more recent experience of the Rudd–Gillard government. Both prime ministers were subjected to campaigns of extreme aggression. Rudd was attacked by business over his mining tax, in the most savage display of corporate ferocity in decades. During Gillard's time in power, the Murdoch papers, which had seemed already to have reached a frenzy, became still more extreme, abetted by misogynistic attacks and an emboldened business lobby. Gillard's minority government was routinely described as "illegitimate." The Liberals, meanwhile, clearly felt they were a government-in-waiting; that they were the only proper holders of power in the country.

When Albanese, who was a senior minister and then deputy prime minister in those governments, talks about wanting Labor to be the "natural party of government," this is the history he is pushing back against. More than that, it is the constant sense that Labor is somehow inadequate. It is, perhaps, not just a perception but a feeling he is trying to expunge.

*

This may be why defeat stings Labor so badly. It is not *only* failure, which is demoralising enough; not only the lost chance to do more of what the party thinks is good, to stop its opponents from doing what it thinks is bad. When the Liberals lose, they know in their bones they will be back: that is their destiny. When MPs from a Labor government lose, rejected by the people, it is as though they have been told, again, that they are not up to the job; that they *don't belong*; that they have failed in their attempt to pass as people who know how to govern. Once upon a time, this was a matter of class. It has been many years since Labor ranks were dominated by the working classes – but then, feelings have little to do with logic.

This might help explain one of the remarkable features of the modern Labor Party: how quickly and brutally it disposes of its heroes. After Gough Whitlam's fall, political journalist Paul Kelly has written, the party devoted itself to two tasks: avoiding Whitlam's economic failure and matching the ruthlessness of Malcolm Fraser. After Keating went, Don Watson wrote, the party ran up "a new flag and will sail anywhere including the doldrums or over the horizon and out of sight to steer clear of the recent past. The new imperative is – do nothing that might remind the people of Keating."

More recently, Labor has done everything it can to make sure voters know this new era is nothing like the Rudd–Gillard era.

*

I understand that sense of shame; of being part of what was perceived by many, in its immediate aftermath, as a failure. I spent years attacking myself for the mistakes I had made as a Labor staffer, the things I had and had not done. So I well understand why, given the chance to redo history, to take another path, Labor wants to try it.

In fact, the best way to understand the approach of the Albanese government may be as a reaction to the Rudd–Gillard experience. The gradualism comes from the desire for long-term government; and the desire for long-term government is the major lesson drawn from the Rudd–Gillard years. If you don't have a long-term government, the argument runs, you cannot guarantee policies will stick. In 2023, Albanese told party members, "We know what we have begun can be undone unless we are there to protect it."

The argument makes intuitive sense. But does it hold up? There are two objections. The first is that this idea of "embedding" policy depends on passing legislation and letting it become part of the landscape. But this would seem to depend on passing it early, and we are now almost four years into the life of this government.

The other objection is stronger still. Which policies of the Rudd–Gillard years, exactly, were lost, outside of the carbon price? Albanese argues the NDIS and NBN were mismanaged by the Liberals – but the weakness of this argument is telling, because obviously both policies survive today. In fact, much of the Albanese government's time has been spent doing further work on the policies of Rudd and Gillard: the NDIS, the NBN, the Gonski education reforms.

The fact this government is in substantive respects a continuation of that one suggests that you can deliver a significant number of enduring policies in a short time, as long as they're good policies.

Medicare is given as the major parable for the importance of long-term government. Medicare was introduced by Whitlam (as "Medibank"), effectively torn down by Malcolm Fraser, then revived by Bob Hawke. The argument made is that Hawke's long reign was necessary to embed Medicare. But this argument, superficially convincing, conveniently skips over the fact that the policy returned from the Whitlam years. Again, we come to the conclusion: the ideas matter at least as much, if not more.

*

But ideas can get you into trouble. And trouble is the very last thing this government wants.

This is a complicated subject, because it can be hard to draw a line between reasonable response and emotional overcompensation. It is not unreasonable to have lived through the Rudd–Gillard years and drawn the conclusion that to change the balance of power in society you must proceed slowly, carefully, cleverly. But it is hard not to wonder, sometimes, if this government has learnt the lesson a little too well. To wonder whether – because the lesson comes with helpings of shame and sadness – the MPs who lived through that time, who dominate the cabinet, go too far out of their way to avoid the slightest hint of anything that might remind them of those years.

The most scarring of Labor's battles in that era – apart from the internal ones – were with business. So it would make sense if you discovered, in the Albanese government's aversion to conflict, a pattern of avoiding fights with business in particular.

Which you do. Not, it should be said, in every case. Labor held its ground against the powerful Pharmacy Guild. Earlier this year, in one of his strongest statements of belief, Albanese made it clear he would not back down on industrial relations: "I'm a Labor prime minister and I support penalty rates. I'm a Labor prime minister and I support real wages increasing. I'm a Labor prime minister and I support an economy that works for people, not people working for an economy."

And yet the pattern is still striking. We have already touched on the concessions given by the government in its dealings with banks, supermarkets, gas and gaming companies. There is the support given to Qantas, despite its atrocious treatment of both customers and workers. In 2024, Albanese attacked the Liberals and Greens for being anti-capitalist, effectively casting Labor as the guardian of the capitalist system in its current form. In September that same year, the prime minister, when criticised by the Business Council for the government's industrial relations changes, reassured everyone that Labor and business were "in sync on what the priorities are."

The habit is most jarring on climate policy. We export a staggering amount of fossil fuels; we are – a stunning fact, surely – in the top five largest exporters in the world. This Labor government continues to subsidise the companies involved, giving away billions of dollars. In September it gave approval to Woodside's extension of the North West Shelf gas project until 2070 – forty-five years from now.

You could expand this line of inquiry further, to policies that don't affect large businesses. In its first term the government announced a new tax regime for those with large superannuation balances. The Senate wouldn't pass it, so the government took it to the election. After the election, Labor had the numbers to pass its laws – but after pushback, most particularly from *The Australian Financial Review* and *The Australian*, it changed its policy in a substantial retreat.

Again and again, it is those with assets who are protected. The schools to which the wealthy send their children are allowed to continue discriminating against LGBTQIA+ people. The wealthy can keep a huge portion of their tax cut. The value of homes – for owner-occupiers and investors alike – will be protected. When we say this government does not like conflict, this mostly means it does not want conflict with those who have assets.

We have here a return to the declared powerlessness of "achievable." As Richard Denniss wrote this year, in an essay on the perils of centrism: "When a person, a party, or a country makes it clear that it will always be willing to compromise then it will always fall victim to those who insist they will not give an inch. Indeed, once someone declares they will always be happy to meet others in the middle they give their opponents an incentive to drive a hard bargain." This is the danger of always insisting on consensus, or that you need bipartisan support, or that you will always listen to those who don't like your views.

The other lesson Labor has over-learnt from the Rudd–Gillard era is about the danger of internal conflict. Again, this is not entirely without reason – and yet it's possible Labor has missed the more important lesson. The problem, initially, wasn't the disunity that became such a problem later on. What preceded the explosion of madness that saw Rudd taken down was almost the precise opposite: the too-long suppressed fear, in an overly acquiescent ministry, of challenging both the style and substance of a dominant, electorally successful leader.

This is the nature of shame. It stops you seeing the past clearly – which then gets in the way of seeing the present.

*

If Labor is repeating its old trick of striding away from its most recent predecessors because of what it myopically sees as their failures, what is it moving towards? The answer to this is easy. It is the glittering memory of the Hawke–Keating success.

Graham Freudenberg once described Labor as "a collective memory in action." That collective memory, driven by emotion, has inevitably harked back to Labor's longest period in government: a period in which Labor won the approval of the Australian people at five successive elections, and for which it has since garnered such praise, including from its usual critics.

What else marked that period? Hawke wanted good processes – as Albanese does. On being elected, Hawke spoke of bringing "calmness and a sense of assuredness" – which Albanese too has brought. In the words of the journalist Mike Steketee, "It did not sound like a revolution, socialist or otherwise, and that was precisely Hawke's intention." Sound familiar?

Part of the way Hawke was able to sustain this impression was the way his government worked with business. He prized consensus. At times he pursued changes which business railed against, but it is also true that his government, with Paul Keating as treasurer, pursued what was becoming the new economic thinking: it put an enormous focus on markets; it deregulated; privatised; promoted globalisation and competition. One of the reasons the Left criticised Hawke at the time was that his personal closeness to businessmen confirmed its suspicions that Labor itself was becoming too close to business, too enamoured of big business's view of how the country should be run.

Hawke and Keating are both Labor heroes for good reason. Their governments introduced Medicare; saved the Franklin River; acted on the High Court's land rights judgments. They are remembered for many achievements that are obviously Labor-tinted. But they are not only lionised by the left. They are frequently held up as heroes by the papers of Australia's arch-capitalists, *The Australian* and *The Australian Financial Review*. Hawke (when he was alive) and Keating would no doubt say that is understandable: their reforms delivered huge economic growth. But it is also true that Labor, under Hawke and Keating, delivered reforms the right would have been proud of. We know this because, as Howard's attempts in the years since to claim joint credit for them demonstrate, the right *is* proud of them. This should perhaps cause Labor to pause and consider how, precisely, to think about that legacy.

Immediately after 1996, Labor erased Keating from its history. That was a mistake. But it is possible it has made another mistake in the years since. It can feel, often, with the Albanese government's emphasis on working with business, the premium it places on consensus, its insistence that it believes in markets, that it is the neoliberal aspects of the Hawke–Keating government that have come to loom so large in Labor's collective memory: the economically rational Keating, whose policies were shepherded through by the consensus, business-friendly Hawke.

At issue is not whether Labor's policies were good or bad. Paul Keating ferociously rejects the "neoliberal" label, pointing to the reforms Labor brought in alongside those elements: Medicare and superannuation. This points to the more important question for Labor as it moves into the future: the choice of which elements of that successful government to emphasise in its collective memory.

In fact, it is possible for Labor to hold onto the Hawke and Keating who deregulated the economy – not by hewing to the ideology behind those changes, with all their benefits for business, but by recapturing their spirit: the sense of adventure and imagination, the idea that assumptions about the way things were could be abandoned, a new world built.

The remarkable fact is that Labor, which has historically been so good at mythologising its past, has in this case effectively allowed the right to choose what will dominate its collective memory.

*

Keating's attempts to bring a new world into being point to a frequent absence in Albanese's rhetoric. Asked early this year what "fighting Tories" meant, Albanese said it was "not giving up gains that have been made." Consider what the prime minister could have said: that he liked changing the country against determined opposition; that he liked to win political fights in order to create grand Labor projects. Instead, he said he wanted *not to give up* something that was already in place.

This theme is echoed in his description of the "Australian way," which began with talk of what he wanted to *prevent* Australia from becoming: "We don't want our health system to be more American. We don't need to copy the ideologies of any other nation."

These are the opposite of promises to make things happen; they are, instead, promises to stop things from happening, to keep Australia as it is. As others have noted, Labor has cast itself as a version of what the conservatives once were: the defender of the way things are.

This may well appeal to large numbers of Australians, as it did in this last election. Election victories, though, while undeniably essential, are not measures of whether the things Labor judges worthwhile are being done – otherwise Labor must accept that John Howard and Scott Morrison were taking the country along the right track. Labor's task, historically, has been to change things on behalf of those who desperately need them to change.

Albanese's most common description of his government's focus – holding nobody back and leaving nobody behind – is clearly Labor in its sentiments. And yet even here we find the rhetoric is about what we must not allow to happen. There is, as so often with this government, a reluctance to state clearly, in sharp and positive language, what it wants to achieve.

This may be because the phrase itself holds a contradiction at its heart. Every time an "aspirational" policy is supported with taxpayer money – tax breaks for home ownership, tax breaks for investment properties, the tax deductibility of private school donations, public funding for private schools, tax breaks for the superannuation of the rich – those dollars cannot go elsewhere. The genuinely poor must continue living in poverty. Public school students must wait a decade for decent funding. Houses remain unaffordable to those without rich parents.

Not holding anyone back and not leaving anyone behind are worthy sentiments. But leaving society largely as it is means the second of those sentiments is treated as less important than the first.

It is largely forgotten now that Albanese didn't get to his "Absolutely" declaration on the minimum wage immediately. Asked that morning, he seemed to hedge – he was supportive, but said the Fair Work Commission made its own decisions. When he did say something clear later that day, "Absolutely" immediately became a source of controversy: the conservative and business press jumped on it. But Albanese stuck to his commitment, and the line became one of the most memorable moments of that campaign.

During his next campaign, in 2025, Albanese had no such unscripted moment. But he did have an equally memorable line, the one about doing things "the Australian way"; not perhaps a hugely striking phrase in its own right but powerful because of the context in which it was delivered, Donald Trump having recently caused global chaos with his developing trade war.

By election night, it had become so prominent among campaign themes that Albanese began and ended his victory speech with it. But, as with "Absolutely," he had to build to it. An early version of the sentiment had appeared in a speech before the campaign. Slowly, these references to a uniquely Australian approach – "Australian policy for Australian conditions" – became more common and more elaborate, until they were one of the clearest things Albanese had to say about his own agenda. Early in his second term it acquired a label: "progressive patriotism."

One question raised by these twin campaign declarations is to do with time. If we accept Albanese's public comments as indicative of his beliefs (if not conclusive), this still leaves an open question: which Albanese should we take to be the true one? The one who was reluctant to give a clear answer on whether he supported a specific pay rise, or the one who said, "Absolutely"? The one who briefly highlighted the Australianness of Medicare, or the one who argued for a specifically Australian way of governing, complete with title and extended definition?

The question is more complex than it first appears. Did Albanese change between the first statement and the second? Or was he merely holding back a belief he was already sure of, developing the confidence to declare it publicly and forthrightly?

In our own lives, it is some combination of these options. Most of us are not philosophers; we have not sat down and worked out precisely what it is we believe about the way the world operates or should operate. Instead, something impels us to speak. Words come out. We hear ourselves say them and, as we do, decide whether to proceed or turn back. If we like what we hear, and if people whom we respect also seem to like what they hear, then we might be encouraged to say more; the more we say, the more we understand of what we believe. Albanese is likely feeling his way towards these positions in the same way we do.

Is that reasonable, though, for a politician? Aren't they in a similar category to philosophers – isn't this what they do for a living?

*

In a book I wrote about Scott Morrison, I pointed out the emptiness of Morrison's beliefs with reference to his describing Australia as "an ideology":

> This is the most extreme expression of contentment and complacency imaginable. So satisfied is Morrison with Australia as it is that he believes it constitutes its own belief system. If you believe in Australia right now, in its current state, then that will overwhelm all else. This is not a country that is becoming, but a country that has arrived at its state of perfection. It is the promised land.

If there is a difference between Morrison's formulation of Australia as an ideology and Albanese's "Australian way," it lies in the fact the Labor man connects this Australianness to a particular policy, a distinctively Labor policy: Medicare. And we know how Albanese feels about Australia's health system, because on several occasions – including when announcing the date of the 2025 election – he has recalled that when his mother became ill she was taken to the same room at Royal Prince Alfred Hospital that Kerry Packer stayed in after his famous heart attack. Albanese has used that story to talk about the importance of universalism: the principle that everyone in a society should have access to a necessary service, in this case healthcare. In other words, the vagueness of the formulation is given weight by being anchored to a specific principle tied to a specific policy, just as his declaration that the minimum wage should rise was only given heft by his committing to the figure of 5.1 per cent.

Action is the way that ideals cross the bridge from being only words to becoming recognisable beliefs.

*

There are days I despair of this government, thinking these people are wasting their precious chance. Sometimes, on X (formerly Twitter), a list will be circulated, by fervent Labor supporters, designed to persuade doubters of just how much the government has achieved. I have read several of these, and each time I find that reading the list has the opposite effect to that intended.

Other days I think, suddenly, that I am being unreasonable – demanding too much. I remind myself that urgent care clinics help people, that paid parental leave is genuinely important, that it is good that gig workers have been given more rights.

I know I am not alone in bouncing back and forth between these views.

Sometimes I think the gap is between what it must feel like to be inside a government looking out, and outside a government looking in. Inside, you are under siege. You see the guns pointing at you and must find a way to protect yourself. Survival and appeasement become your priority. You begin to believe that whatever you are doing is all you can do – and, what's more, it is exactly what you should be doing.

The day after an election is when those two perspectives are most likely to converge. Except for hardcore partisans who hate the party that wins, the nation comes together; we have taken part in a joint project of choosing this government. For a moment, its stories are our own, because we have accepted those stories to justify our choice. The day after the 2025 election, I wrote:

> On Saturday, for the first time, it was possible to glimpse what few besides Albanese himself have understood. That is, how different Australia may look after several terms of a Labor government. Over his 11 years in power, Howard articulated a version of Australia to itself, matched it with policies and became a kind of personification of his era. After Saturday, it is possible to ask whether Albanese has begun to do the same for these times.

In other words, I found myself believing, again, both that Albanese had a vision of a kinder, fairer country, and that he might achieve it. On that day I could see the fuller meaning of his belief that Labor should be the natural party of government: that the values he ascribes to Labor, of fairness and caring for those who need it, are, if not the best description of Australia, a description of the best possible Australia; and that by presenting this portrait of us to ourselves for nine years or more he could bring it closer to becoming a reality.

One of Albanese's responses to the charge of timidity is that his government has in fact been bold: that it is a government just like other Labor governments, every bit as brave, mistakenly criticised in the same ways they were. But then at other times he has responded by saying he wants his government to last, apparently conceding that his government is not so bold after all. In the moments I doubt my confusion, I can remind myself: the government seems as confused on this point as I am.

Perhaps it is true that voters no longer expect "something more" from Labor. But if so, isn't this a mistake – shouldn't we all expect more of our governments, of whatever political stripe? And more still from Labor, which has, at least historically, promised more?

This is always frustrating for Labor leaders. You can tell it frustrates Albanese. Once he was outside, looking in, wanting Labor to do more. Now he is inside, arguing that he is doing all he can.

But we know that Albanese understands the inextinguishable desire for more, because he has said so. Halfway through his first term, he was asked what progressives are progressing towards – what was the endpoint? "Well, there is no endpoint, by definition," he said. "It means you constantly progress and move forward." His interviewer pressed him: to what – a mythical nirvana?

"No, no, to a more inclusive society. To one that has greater opportunity regardless of people's birth or people's ethnicity or religion or gender. A country that is able to move forward as a whole, but an economy, for example, that works for everyone, not people working for an economy."

This is one of Albanese's clearest articulations of his vision for the country. Sometimes, you hear it.

*

Incrementalism does not have to equal lack of belief. It is possible that a politician knows exactly what he wants to do – but has decided, as Albanese says so often, that he must bring people with him, step by small step. Jim Chalmers puts it this way: "My theory of governing is people will cop big things done slowly and little things done quickly, but not big things done quickly or little things done slowly."

The Americans Aubrey Fox and Greg Berman recently published a book in defence of incrementalism, which they argue can bring about large change through the accretion of small changes over time. This is more or less what Albanese says, too; he told me in 2023 that your impression of the government's pace depended on whether you saw it as a long-term government, the implication being that what doesn't initially seem impressive might build into significant achievement.

He has a point. Sometimes, when totting up a past government's early successes, we say it commenced a series of reforms – the importance of the first move having become clear only in hindsight. This is an argument you could make, say, about Labor's large-scale changes to superannuation, which took years. In 2022, its architects, Paul Keating and Bill Kelty, spoke to journalists at *The Australian Financial Review*. Kelty said:

> Paul said we gotta make up our mind what we are, and what we want to do with super … we don't want to be tinkerers or reformers …

> It was that day in late 1984 that we reached agreement in principle. We will be revolutionaries. We will change the system. But we will not tear down the existing system. We will build a new system.

For Keating, this was part of his broader vision; he said that, as treasurer:

> I had to essentially take on and change the implicit standings of the whole labour movement … I had to take the whole model on. I was blessed with time because we won in '83, '84, '87 and me in '93. But I never wasted a second, I never wasted a minute. You have really got to want to do this stuff.

Of course, we should be wary of treating the narratives of Keating and Kelty with too much credulity; they are telling the tale forty years after the fact. Government is often a matter of improvisation. Afterwards, when your time in power is over, it is time to tell the story of what you have done. And this is the way Keating and Kelty narrate their successes: as grand schemes planned in advance. But here is journalist Paul Kelly, writing in 1992 about the government's broader economic agenda: "Virtually every economic milestone in the early years was a response to a crisis … Hawke and Keating were improvisers … The story of their government … is that of managers having to combat huge shocks imposed from abroad."

A similar point has often been made about Roosevelt's New Deal, an era-altering collection of policies. One former adviser wrote, "To look upon these programs as the result of a unified plan was to believe that the accumulation of stuffed snakes, baseball pictures, school flags, old tennis shoes, carpenter's tools, geometry books, and chemistry sets in a boy's bedroom could have been put there by an interior decorator."

Jim Chalmers, like Keating, talks of not wasting time. He will stop meetings to get people to listen to the clock in his office ticking. "I'm *petrified* of getting to the end of the day and not having made the most of it," he has said. We may not yet know exactly what he wants to do with all that time – but perhaps that is only because there is still time ahead of him in which to improvise.

Is it possible, then, to see the Albanese government's approach to governing in general – to the actual policies it will pursue – as akin to the way Albanese worked his way towards "Absolutely" and "progressive patriotism"? This would fit with something Albanese told journalist Katharine Murphy for Quarterly Essay 88: "Action, reaction, action, reaction. Are we where we need to be?"

The difficulty with expecting politicians to have a set of fixed beliefs is that, like each of us, they must live in the world and respond to that world as it changes. If beliefs exist in our external actions, as Dennett suggests – rather than in some secret chamber of our hearts – then it is inevitable they will shift.

Viewed like this, Albanese's declaration that he does have strong beliefs but is also open to changing them doesn't sound cynical or ridiculous; it sounds reasonable. It sounds human.

*

There are three obvious ways we might come to see this government in the future – each very much still possible. The first is that what appears to be its gradualism will, over time, reveal itself as a reasonably significant agenda that has been accumulating, missed in the moment by a hollowed-out media. The second is that Albanese will, sometime in his prime ministership, break free of this approach; become a bold, visionary, fighting prime minister. At that moment, we will stop and realise: ah, this is what it's all been for, this biding of time, this building of trust. The third is that the current approach will continue and turn out to be what critics of the government already suggest: a series of opportunities missed by a reasonably competent but ultimately underwhelming outfit that chose to continue meekly along the path set by previous governments rather than finding its own.

And then there is a fourth potential verdict, less obvious. Lately, I have sometimes had an image in my mind, one that will likely seem incongruous. It is of Albanese as Perseus.

In the first of his *Six Memos for the Next Millennium*, the Italian novelist Italo Calvino spoke of the quality of "lightness." His archetype was Perseus, of the winged sandals, who goes to battle Medusa, the snake-haired Gorgon whom no human could look at without turning to stone. Therefore, Perseus only ever looks at her reflection in his bronze shield. Later, after he has cut off her head, he keeps the head with him, in a sack; he can force others to look at her – turning them to stone – but avoids looking himself.

Calvino doesn't quite say so, but in his telling Medusa symbolises the world, with its endless succession of events and tragedies. He says of the Greek hero:

> Perseus succeeds in mastering that horrendous face by keeping it hidden, just as in the first place he vanquished it by viewing it in a mirror. Perseus's strength always lies in a refusal to look directly, but not in a refusal of the reality in which he is fated to live; he carries the reality with him and accepts it as his particular burden.

Albanese is a little like Perseus, isn't he? He carries the world with him: he cannot escape it. For six months after he was elected for a second time, he was dogged by questions about when he would meet Trump; for two years, the debate on Gaza has followed him around. He has not entirely avoided these issues; but nor has he quite looked directly at them. When thousands of Australians joined protests against immigration organised by the far right, Albanese deplored the role of neo-Nazis. But he also said there would have been "good people" there. Instead of condemning all the protesters, he urged them to consider whom they stood with.

I am sceptical of this approach: my feeling is that a prime minister should be unequivocal in such moments. But I could be wrong. What Albanese did, as so often, was refuse to get weighed down, stuck; instead, he touched down briefly to deliver his message and left again on his journey, using his energy where it was useful.

It is possible to perceive a similar lightness in Albanese's method of distancing our country from its unthinking closeness to the United States.

Journalist Shaun Carney argues this is being done in three ways: first, Albanese is forging a closer relationship with China. Second, he is publicly rejecting calls to increase defence spending to America's desired amount. Third, he has recognised Palestinian statehood, against US wishes. Like Hawke and Keating, he is responding to a series of huge shocks from abroad, improvising as he goes.

Unlike Hawke and Keating, he is doing this slowly, stealthily. In part, this is the approach determined by the subject matter: diplomacy is by definition required. But as Carney writes, it is his style, as well. Like Perseus, he carries reality with him, while keeping his glance trained somewhere else.

And perhaps this is the way to view Albanese's approach more broadly. What is clearer in relation to racist rallies and America may be true of other, less controversial topics too. Remember that Labor's recent election victory was, in the words of the party's national president, Wayne Swan, "wide but shallow," built on a low primary vote – and that in such heated times large reforms, likely to attract outsized attention from the media, split voters into sides. In such a perilous environment, it might make sense that the centre-left treads delicately. That Albanese chooses, instead of large, cumbersome changes, comparatively light ones: changes that do not get weighed down by controversy but that bit by bit, as he says himself, demonstrate that government can improve people's lives.

To switch metaphors: perhaps the way to think about all this is that Albanese is walking slowly across a rope bridge that leads from one side of this fascism-prone era to the other; that it is enough if he gets to the other side.

*

But there is also a risk to this strategy of lightness, one that became apparent in Albanese's first term, as Labor's polling numbers fell amid the pain caused by inflation – and which election victory should not make Labor forget.

The danger with incrementalism is that it is politics as vicious circle. You are concerned – as Albanese repeatedly tells us he is – about the public's cynicism towards politics. This means you can't attempt large things, because they might fail and provoke more cynicism. So you do small things that seem more likely to succeed. But because they are so small, nobody notices them – which only breeds cynicism about the effectiveness of government.

And then there is another danger, which is that the things you are doing are not grand enough or bold enough to work. The government is currently not on track to meet its home-building target; the Reserve Bank governor said she did not think government efforts would "have any impact in the next two years." While there are different views, many experts believe the government will not meet its 2030 emissions reduction target, nor its renewable energy target.

With time, too, people begin to notice things you said you'd do, but simply haven't. In Opposition, Labor complained loudly about Scott Morrison's changes to university fees, which have made arts degrees – often studied by more disadvantaged university entrants – ridiculously expensive. At the time of writing there are no clear plans to act. Labor retreated on its superannuation changes. There is confusion about what the government plans to do about its commitment to the remaining elements of the Uluru Statement from the Heart.

*

You can never really know what to make of a government until its time in office ends. Until then, it holds great potential both to achieve and disappoint.

A lot can happen even in three years. The government's first term was not just one thing. The second year, in particular, stood out: that was when it did the hard stuff. Albanese campaigned for the Indigenous Voice to Parliament and broke his promise on the stage-three tax cuts. That left a year before the election, in which the government could try to put any difficulties behind it while luring voters back with targeted promises.

Prime ministers get into habits. Albanese has already labelled this the "Year of Delivery," meaning keeping the government's election pledges. This has a similar feel to the first year of his first term. It is possible this second term will follow the same trajectory: that in about six months we will see the government again take up difficult causes; that for that middle year of three it will break free of the straitjacket in which it has placed itself.

But I am conscious, too, that with incrementalism the date of judgement always seems to be somewhere down the track. This is a useful tool for fobbing off journalists and critics – anyone, really, who suggests the government should get a move on: patience, please!

If Labor MPs want more from their time in government than to stay in power, this political convenience may also be a trap. They can tell themselves things are happening; that change is building; they only need to wait. But it is also possible that, on the day that they lose power, they find themselves still waiting.

We should take seriously the possibility that Australia's future is not the bright one politicians like to promise. Twenty-seven years ago, Richard Rorty described the US Democratic Party leaving behind "any mention of distribution, and moving into a sterile vacuum called the 'center.' The party no longer has a visible, noisy left wing … It is as if the distribution of income and wealth had become too scary a topic for any [politician] ever to mention." Rorty then predicts America's future. As social mobility falls, an overclass comes to run the country. The super-rich operate the economy, leaving politicians to fight over cultural issues. Those outside the white-collar overclass despair of the system and elect a strongman. The gains made by minorities go. "Jocular contempt for women will come back into fashion." Racial slurs spread.

Recall Andrew Leigh's warning that we are a generation away from American-style inequality. Our political class tends to think we are protected by compulsory voting. But what if, in fact, we are merely twenty or so years behind America?

Quinn Slobodian has written about the trend of countries establishing economic "zones" in which exceptions to their laws are permitted, in order to entice businesses. Duty-free zones were the very modest beginning; slowly, such zones spread across the world – capitalist utopias, some the size of large cities, where the rich can run businesses as they like, treat workers as they like, while the rest of the country, a few kilometres away, carries on as usual.

This is easy to miss in a country like Australia, which feels relatively unified. Increasingly, the world is splitting – being split – into thousands of jurisdictions. The rich can move between them; the movement of the poor, meanwhile, is more and more stringently controlled. There is even, Slobodian records, a "seasteading" movement, in which "aquapreneurs" build new cities atop the unregulated ocean. If you are rich, you can, in effect, start your own country.

This is not so alien to the Australian experience after all. Very briefly in a late stage of the pandemic, I found myself living in a small one-bedroom apartment with my partner and our one-year-old. Each of us got COVID; for two weeks we were entirely confined to this space. I cannot now visit that suburb without feeling a shudder of dread. Some people, I know, lived for years that way. In contrast, during the pandemic, one Sydney businessman told a podcast that he had, with all this time on his hands, discovered rooms in his house he had never been in before.

This is a simple contrast between wealth and less wealth. But it tells us something about what wealth enables, which is escape. There are two halves to escape. You must want to escape *from* somewhere, and have somewhere to escape *to*. The reason this became visible during the pandemic was because, suddenly, we all needed to escape, but only some of us had a destination available, be it in our own house or down the coast somewhere, or perhaps in another state, or another country: another jurisdiction. Wealth effectively allowed many to secede from the pandemic.

And this, in turn, is a particularly concrete version of the fundamental division in this neoliberal era, which points back towards its propagandised version. "Freedom!" is the cry that has gone up since Reagan and Thatcher made this their theme. Their genius was to thread freedom through different spaces. Freedom of markets, freedom from control, freedom of choice. "Freedom of choice?" It should be remembered that much of this "freedom" requires money. You have the freedom to send your child to whatever type of school you like – if you can pay. You have the freedom to pick your doctor – if you can pay. And so on.

Once again, the rich can go anywhere.

And the rest of us? Consider, these days, the intense regulation of so much of our lives. Consider in particular the ways in which work is expanding. Many of us are on call, all the time – despite the recent laws. Work comes to our phones, our homes. Those in the gig economy are often working several jobs, with little security. And alongside this, employers are surveilling us in increasingly sophisticated ways.

The rich can go anywhere, the poor can go nowhere.

Two points come from this. The first is that, as Slobodian writes, capitalism and democracy are diverging – on the right's terms. The United States offers a glaring example. As Trump destroys its democratic institutions and strips back accountability, capitalism is thriving: Trump has made billions from his presidency and, for much of that time at least, the stock market has continued to climb. Having taken what they can from the intertwining of capitalism and democracy, the super-rich now seek to depart; capitalism, having sucked democracy dry, now seeks greener pastures.

The staggering fact about all this is that, as Daniel Immerwahr writes in a review of Slobodian's work, the rich are not satisfied with their freedoms: "They live in compounds, fly on private jets, sail superyachts, hoard art in free ports, buy islands, found online worlds, build bunkers, establish alternative currencies, or launch themselves into space." Which leaves us with this difficulty: "Government by loophole makes for a cynical society where shared values are transparent fictions and collective action is daunting. It's hard to know, in a zone-riddled world, how problems requiring coordination and shared sacrifice could be solved."

This is the second point: that marshalling the collective will to do something about the problems created by this extreme version of neoliberalism is becoming ever more difficult.

If aquapreneurs and economic zones sound a little futuristic – even though such zones are abundant – another way to think of the divergence of democracy and capitalism lies in your local area. As Slobodian points out, there is such a thing as "soft-secession," "opting out of society" through private schools, gated communities and siloed media environments. The private health system is part of this too. Even GPs – part of our prized universal health system – are increasingly divided by price. The rich and the poor in Australia live different lives in different places. In a country with such tangible divisions, how can a government hope to create consensus around the idea of significant change?

None of this has to lead to revolution, or even to utopianism. I think the writer and art historian T.J. Clark is correct when he says that a belief in utopias can be a way to avoid looking at reality. And yet seeing reality with clarity demands an act of imagination. We cannot see our world as it is – what is lacking, the ways it is failing us – unless we can imagine it being some other way.

Clark defends gradualism: "a politics of small steps, bleak wisdom, concrete proposals, disdain for grand promises, a sense of the hardness of even the least 'improvement.'" This is, for the most part, a fair description of Albanese's project. But Clark's next sentence is crucial: "It depends on what the small steps are aimed at changing."

This government is not rudderless. It wants to help workers and make sure we all have access to healthcare and childcare. While valuable, these seem like incremental additions to what we have already. Clark argues that what is needed is "a piece-by-piece, assumption-by-assumption dismantling of the politics we have." What, then, is Labor dismantling?

Albanese has put two of our national assumptions up for grabs. One, very tentatively: Australia's relationship with America. The tentativeness is perhaps appropriate for the magnitude of the task: as my old colleague from Rudd's office, Lachlan Harris, wrote in these pages, the leader who charts our country's "post-American future" will "join the ranks of Australia's truly great prime ministers."

Second, Albanese wishes to put "kindness" at the centre of the Australian project, by convincing Australians that Labor values are the best description of the country. If actually practised, this would involve a radical shift from the years in which John Howard urged us to be "relaxed and comfortable" – and a dismantling of the attitudes and assumptions of neoliberalism.

In 2024, Robert D. Putnam, the author of *Bowling Alone*, outlined three factors that run in parallel to the loss of community. One is political polarisation; another is inequality; and a third is culture, the very neoliberal idea that it is every man for himself. But what is "upstream of all these other trends," he said, "is morality, a sense that we're all in this together and that we have obligations to other people. Now, suddenly, I'm no longer the social scientist, I'm a preacher. I'm trying to say, we're not going to fix polarization, inequality, social isolation until, first of all, we start feeling we have an obligation to care for other people. And that's not easy, so don't ask me how to do that."

Putnam is right: the task is both essential and difficult. And so perhaps Albanese has come along at exactly the right time, with his stubborn determination to persuade us that one of our national values is kindness. In the effort to convince citizens to take on the obligation of caring for others, having a prime minister willing to make that case – to state this particular belief of his out loud – gives Australia a large head-start.

But Albanese is in politics, which means he has the power to do things that actually make this a kinder country. This will involve a similar determination to that which Keating and Kelty showed in building a whole new system. If his intention is to drag us into a new era, in which the ethos of the neoliberal era is replaced by something better, then he will need not only to assert such values but to alter the structures and policies which run against those values. It might be that fixing inequality is "downstream" of morality. But Albanese can only coax us along the path to a new morality. He can actually *do* something about inequality.

*

The layout of the prime minister's office, who sat where, the light, the pace at which I walked: all are as firmly fixed in my memory as any detail of my life. To enter the media office from the rest of the office, there was a heavy swing door that had to be pushed. I would lean on it, often with my shoulder, and swing my way in. This motion took just enough time for a thought to arrive, then depart. In the days leading up to my decision to leave, I would think, each time I pushed that door, of writing, of having the time to write. I think I barely knew what I would write. But that was the thought.

Since then, I have discovered what anyone who writes will tell you: that the essence of the experience is failure. You have some bright, shining idea; you work to commit it to paper; inevitably, it fails to match the vision in your mind.

In his short book *The Hatred of Poetry*, Ben Lerner writes:

> the poet is a tragic figure. The poem is always a record of failure. There is an "undecidable conflict" between the poet's desire to sing an alternative world and, as [Allan] Grossman puts it, the "resistance to alternative making inherent in the materials of which any world must be composed."

The same is true of politics in general, and the politics of the left in particular.

Left politics carries in it the sense of what might be achieved. It is utopian: not in the sense "utopian politics" has come to mean, with a sinister social program waiting to be enacted, but utopian in its broadest sense, the idea that there is a utopia of some sort that it is possible for us to begin building. Of course, it can't ever be completed; there is no heaven on earth.

The history of left politics, then, is a record of failure. And yet these days, so often, it is talked about only in terms of success. Take the Voice referendum, the way it seems already to be fading from history, Indigenous affairs becoming invisible, as though Albanese's bold decision to push forward with that vote is only a cause for regret, to be written out of Labor's story.

Or take Keating: what is recalled now is the floating of the dollar, the deregulation of the economy. But what about Keating's failures: the failure to deliver a republic, a new flag? The failure to change Australia's conception of its security? The failure to help Australia to grow up? Aren't these failures important, in a different way, from his successes? The ideas they pushed forward still run through our national debate. For now, Howard remains victorious. But the war of ideas is never won with finality. The battles Keating started outlive his prime ministership, just as Whitlam's Medibank did.

Contemporary Labor seems stuck in the narrative of contemporary economics: we must move forward, faster and faster. We must shape ourselves to the incentives of the market. There is no going back; no attempt to recall what once seemed possible, and might again, given that conditions are now different. Labor has become a party which only remembers – only wishes to remember – its successes.

Labor was not always this way. Once, it held up its failures as a type of glory. It's true that you can't govern only in this way – this was part of what was behind Whitlam's declaration that only the impotent are pure. You must have success as well. But there is something valuable in glorifying failure, because failure is the more frequent result when you go up against the odds. Venerating failure is not defeatism, but its opposite: a reminder that hope is essential.

Today's Labor is a graveyard of lost futures with nobody mourning them. Every time something doesn't work, it is discarded. The republic, a new flag, the Voice, seriously challenging the way schools are funded, changes to negative gearing and the capital gains tax, a carbon price and for that matter socialism, whatever that phrase was taken to mean: one by one, possible futures are discarded until Labor is left only with what is already here. And that is because Labor is haunted, too, by the spectre of future failures: seemingly terrified by the potential regret of not achieving what it sets out to do, with the solution being not to attempt much at all.

This narrow view also lacks historical accuracy. Gillard launched her carbon price in the worst possible situation: in minority government, with Rudd behind her, facing into a storm of misogyny. Bill Shorten fought for negative gearing and capital gains tax changes from Opposition. Albanese faces none of these barriers.

It is true that Labor's primary vote remains low by historical standards. But this Labor government has a rare combination of advantages: a huge majority, a prime minister with decades in parliament behind him, experienced ministers, and a united party facing a confused, depleted Opposition. More may be possible than Labor has yet allowed itself to believe.

*

Keating said that politics "will always be about having a conversation with the public." In effect, a leader must listen to voters, but not entirely trust us, when we say "I want X." Instead, their task is to guide us towards a useful conversation, to help us discover, together, what we really want. Inevitably, that process will be difficult; it will meet with significant resistance.

But the rest of us depend on centre-left parties to start such conversations. At a time when belief is breaking down – when we are disillusioned, atomised, exhausted – this role is more important than ever. We do not have time to work out exactly what we believe, not in the specific; and we have no hope of knowing whether what we believe can meaningfully map onto the world. We rely on political parties to have those conversations for us.

Not that this is new. The Italian Marxist philosopher Antonio Gramsci wrote: "One should stress the significance which, in the modern world, political parties have in the elaboration and diffusion of conceptions of the world, because essentially what they do is to work out the ethics and the politics corresponding to these conceptions and act as it were as their historical 'laboratory.'"

Which is very close to language used by Albanese earlier this year, describing the Australia into which John Curtin was born: a "social laboratory." Then, Albanese said, this "spirit of social democratic creativity … ebbed away under conservative governments. Curtin, together with Chifley, gave it new life and meaning."

In other words, governments do not have these necessary conversations with their people only by saying things. We do not listen to governments, not really, until they act. This is how Roosevelt could change his country and the world with such simple advice as this: "Take a method and try it. If it fails, admit it frankly and try another. But above all, try something."

The great difficulty for those governing today is that the entire project of neoliberalism is geared towards avoiding conflict, of a specific type – as Trevor Jackson points out, conflict over resources: "Instead of open conflict over resources and rewards (which is common to other forms of political ideology), liberalism puts its faith in things like education, technology, expertise, and, ultimately, market forces to indefinitely postpone those conflicts."

Albanese's approach matches this perfectly. He avoids conflict, postpones it indefinitely. As long as he does so, he inevitably helps those who benefit from things hewing close to their current condition.

The signs are that we are approaching a point where that postponement becomes untenable. If there is any chance of our society continuing to exist in a way that reflects the "fairness" Albanese says is at the heart of this country, at some point the government will have to significantly intervene in that conflict over resources.

This is an important point, because it is easy to caricature criticisms of our current society as leaving only one option: revolution. Like most people, I don't think revolution is going to happen, and I very much doubt that whatever it brought would be better than what we have. But this is precisely why simply opposing "reformism" to "revolution" gets us nowhere: almost all of us are not revolutionaries. So what? The important questions are different. What type of reform are we talking about? How much? How quickly? We should not allow ourselves to be diverted by Albanese's artificial binary.

To return to Clark one final time: he calls for "inequality and injustice [to] be made again the object of a politics." We have a prime minister from the left wing of his centre-left party; one who grew up working-class; who still has working-class friends. I am certain he believes left-wing things. If a time were to come in which the project of dismantling inequality and injustice took centre-stage, you would expect it to happen under a prime minister like this one.

*

A surprising fact about Labor is that it does, in fact, still indulge in utopianism. Unfortunately, it is the utopianism of neoliberalism, in which technology, harnessed well, will give us everything we want, including a better society. Around the time of the productivity summit, Albanese's economic ministers began talking about an American book, *Abundance*. Its authors begin that book by depicting the future: a world where pills keep you healthy, drones deliver everything, clean and cheap electricity is everywhere. People work less, thanks not only to AI but because the profits from AI have been shared. The authors acknowledge a weakness: "It reads, even to us, as too simple." But conceding the point does not deal adequately with the criticism. They are right: the book is far too simple. Its authors demand we get rid of bad regulations – which will mean more houses and more clean energy projects – and create better processes so that people can invent more and better things.

Sounds fantastic! Alas, this is shallow technological optimism that doesn't seem to grasp how complicated all this is. How do we sort good regulations from bad – the ones that protect the environment effectively, say, from the ones that get in the way of building quickly? Aren't they often the same laws? What role does business play in all this? At times the authors seem to recommend government do more by itself; at others, that private industry be empowered; at others still, that the exact model doesn't matter. It is a hodgepodge that boils down to a simple injunction: make things better. The book is not entirely without merit; some of the questions it raises are worth thinking about. Mostly, though, its message is: fewer regulations and more stuff. It barely touches on redistribution.

Didn't the left already make this mistake once, with the Third Way? Adopting right-wing prescriptions – which its opponents would agree to – and pretending they would achieve left-wing goals? It is an excellent recipe for avoiding conflict. Have all the Labor MPs reading this book admiringly not stopped to wonder, for a moment, why that is?

Consider the list of topics that go unaddressed while the Labor Party is fretting about regulations – topics that are virtually untouchable by mainstream politicians in Australia. The idea that there should be an inheritance tax – which exists in many comparable countries – is too frightening. You simply cannot say that government funding for private schools should be cancelled or even substantially reduced. A Labor prime minister ridicules the idea of breaking up the oligopolistic supermarkets. Private provision of care services – in childcare, in aged care, in disabilities care – has gone horribly awry, yet a genuine alternative seems impossible to canvass. Most tax breaks for the rich are off-limits: capital gains tax exemptions, negative gearing, most superannuation tax concessions. Australia is one of the single largest contributors to global warming through our export of fossil fuels – an amazing statistic that should shame us. Instead of talking about how to wind that back, we are doubling down, opening more gasfields, more coalmines.

And there is an obvious thread running through these taboo topics, so obvious that it barely needs saying: each of these discussions countenances taking wealth away from those who already have it, or restricting the possibility of those with wealth getting still more wealth.

Rather than trying to bring about a better country by constantly avoiding the topics the powerful want us to avoid, a government of the centre-left might consider making those topics its starting point.

As a society, this means asking ourselves what the philosopher Michel Serres (writes Adam Phillips) said is the only modern question: what do we not want to know about ourselves?

That is a question that Labor, too, should consider asking itself. What does it not want to know?

Perhaps that the danger of becoming a natural party of government is that, in accomplishing this task, you become – in both your aims and your methods – essentially conservative. That it is not possible to bring about significant change while also representing the "vast majority of interests," most of which are inevitably invested in things staying as they are.

This is not easy to hear, given Labor's entirely legitimate wish to wield power, but it may also be true that the left, if it is genuinely of the left, can never hold power for long, by definition: that Vere Gordon Childe was right all those many years ago when he pointed to the fundamental contradiction at the heart of parliamentary labour parties. Which means, in turn, that Labor politicians must choose between the legitimacy and longevity they so desperately crave and their knowledge – a deep, felt knowledge – that there are many people who are depending on them (whether those people know it or not) to bring about dramatic change.

And this, too: that as soon as you begin to ask yourself, every day, what is possible, you have begun to curtail the notion of what is possible; you have beckoned the walls, and soon they will begin closing in.

*

In 2009, speaking about the role of music in his life, Paul Keating said:

> The great political leaders have the instincts of artists. This was true of Churchill. There's a logicality to what you do, and always trying to do the greatest things, not the second-best things; always heading for the most sparkling outcome. So I always believe in leadership there are only ever two ingredients: imagination and courage.

I think this idea – that great politicians have much in common with great artists – should be taken seriously. I think it should be taken particularly seriously because of the way we have more lately come to think of politicians: as technocrats, types of elevated bureaucrats. Keating is talking about a particular aspect of making art and of practising politics: seeing beyond what is in front of us and "heading for the most sparkling outcome."

On the cusp of the Albanese government's second year of its second term, a year likely to be decisive in defining the character of this contemporary manifestation of Labor, I will finish by deferring to an artist. The novelist Elena Ferrante has written that "writing is a cage and we enter it right away, with our first line." It is a good sentence to think about in relation to politics. The answer to this dilemma is not to try to break free; rather, it is "to learn to use with freedom the cage we're shut up in." How, then, to exercise freedom within a cage? By adapting and deforming what already exists. Ferrante quotes novelist Ingeborg Bachmann: "We have to work hard with the bad language that we have inherited to arrive at [a new language]."

Elsewhere, Ferrante describes the way she writes; the way she achieves this difficult task. She begins calmly, her prose controlled and contained. Beneath this "cold surface," though, is "a magma of unbearable heat."

The question of Albanese's belief remains perplexing. We can sense in him that magma; we have occasional hints of it in his language and even in his policies. But the surface is cold; he remains contained.

Ferrante says:

> Only when the story begins to emerge safely, thanks to that tone, do I begin to wait for the moment when I'll be able to replace those

> well-oiled, quiet links with something rustier, raspier, and with a pace that's disjointed and agitated, even at the growing risk of the story falling apart. The moment I change register for the first time is both exciting and anguished. I enjoy breaking through my character's armor of good education and good manners. I enjoy upsetting her self-image, her will, and revealing another, rougher soul underneath, someone raucous, maybe even crude. I work hard to make that change in register come as a surprise and also to make it seem natural when we go back to a more serene style of narration.

After establishing a consistent tone, she breaks out of her calmness. There is, she admits, a risk: that the calm will not be able to be recovered or that her readers will no longer believe in that calm. But it is that risk that gives her writing life.

SOURCES

1 "In my 51 years": Ross Gittins, "This election is one of the worst I've seen. Here's the one thing we can do to fix Australian politics", *The Age/Sydney Morning Herald*, 14 April 2025.

1 "Here are two once proud teams": Greg Sheridan, "This is the worst election campaign I've ever seen", *The Australian*, 15 April 2025.

2 "Frankly I think": Peter Dutton, quoted in Paul Karp, "Coalition questions $300 power bill rebate as Chalmers says the wealthy not Labor's 'focus or concern'", *Guardian Australia*, 15 May 2024.

2 warned this was effectively: Peter Dutton, quoted in Tom McIlroy, "Household batteries plan proof power bills will rise under ALP: Dutton", *Australian Financial Review*, 6 April 2025.

2–3 "Labor should be", "I am a progressive", etc.: Anthony Albanese, Media conference (first as leader-elect), Sydney, 27 May 2019.

3 "I want to talk about": Anthony Albanese, RN *Breakfast*, 10 May 2022.

6 "If there is a good predictive model": Anil Gomes,"Tillosophy", *London Review of Books*, 20 June 2024.

7 something puzzling: I think that Paul Strangio, whose short essay on Albanese precedes this one in some respects, is getting at a similar thing when he writes of "a nagging feeling that something was missing" early on in "Is grown-up government enough?", *Inside Story*, 3 September 2024.

7 Years ago: Sean Kelly, "Every parliament's rule of three", *The Saturday Paper*, 29 November 2014.

8 During the Albanese government's first term: Sean Kelly, "If this government is forgettable, Albanese is counting on you remembering the last one", *The Age/Sydney Morning Herald*, 5 August 2024.

8 "the observation that": George Megalogenis, *Minority Report: The new shape of Australian politics*, Quarterly Essay 96, November 2024.

9 "[Man] is a free": Franz Kafka, *The Aphorisms of Franz Kafka*, edited by Reiner Stach, translated by Shelley Frisch, Princeton University Press, 2022, p. 132.

11 "essentially religious": J.M. Coetzee, "Bellow's gift", *The New York Review of Books*, 27 May 2004.

11–12 "There was": Brian McKinlay, *The ALP: A short history of the Australian Labor Party*, Drummond/Heinemann, 1981.

12 "The quality of life": Gough Whitlam, Address to the Annual Conference of the Australian Labor Party (Victorian Branch), 9 June 1967.

12–13 "novel theory of democracy", "surrounded", etc.: Vere Gordon Childe, *How Labour Governs*, Melbourne University Press, 1923.

13 "Opportunism": Mat Reid quoted in Childe, *How Labour Governs.*

13 while deeply influenced by socialism: Frank Bongiorno, "Why does Labor exist?", *Inside Story*, 18 November 2011. I have also relied here on Frank Bongiorno and Nick Dyrenfurth, *A Little History of the Australian Labor Party*, University of New South Wales Press, 2024, in particular pp. 43–51.

13 never been a monolithically socialist party: Don Watson, *Watsonia*, Black Inc., 2020, p. 33.

13–14 "There is no party": Graham Freudenberg in Rodney Cavalier, "A word from the history man", *Australian Financial Review*, 22 December 1988.

14 "To a degree unexpected": McKinlay, *The ALP*, p. 9.

15 "de facto split", "has lost": Strangio, "Is grown-up government enough?".

15 reformist, not a revolutionary: Anthony Albanese, quoted in Troy Bramston, "'I'm a reformist, not a revolutionary,' Anthony Albanese says", *The Australian*, 29 March 2025.

17 "Some of the old ideological divides": Albanese, quoted by Troy Bramston, "'Pragmatic' Albanese declares: Labor faction friction, not on my watch", *The Australian*, 26 September 2025.

17 At the next caucus meeting: Mark Kenny, "Labor is professionalised to the point of pointlessness. Its MPs need to find their voice", *The Canberra Times*, 7 September 2025.

17 In the caucus meeting: Jacob Greber, "Labor's big backbench isn't interested in having a debate", ABC News online, 30 August 2025.

18 "Their loss of patience": Richard Rorty, *Achieving Our Country*, First Harvard University Press, 1999, p. 69.

18 "A plane": John McTernan, "Look out for a reform of the left. It could finally shatter British politics", *The Telegraph*, 10 March 2025.

19 "True believers": Stuart Macintyre, "Who are the true believers?", The Manning Clark Labor History Memorial Lecture, *Labour History*, no. 68, May 1995, pp. 155–67. Macintyre also writes about compromise needing "an informed awareness of what you are yielding" and the potential importance of "doctrinal zeal."

20 "a constellation", "is when": Gary Gerstle, *The Rise and Fall of the Neoliberal Order: America and the world in the free market era*, Oxford University Press, 2022, pp. xiv, 155.

20 "the most radical": Perry Anderson, "Idees-Forces", *New Left Review*, January/ February 2025.

21 "the pressure", "a moral perspective": Gerstle, *The Rise and Fall of the Neoliberal Order*, pp. 11, 2.

21 He has pointed to: Gerstle, talking with Ezra Klein, "Are we on the cusp of a new political order?", *The New York Times*, 1 November 2024.

22 "we're now as unequal": Andrew Leigh, quoted in Patrick Commins, "Andrew Leigh says Australia one generation from 'US-style inequality' as Productivity Commission targets corporate tax", *Guardian Australia*, 19 May 2025.

23 "had the steepest": quoted or paraphrased by Conor Duffy, "Who's to blame for declining school results", *ABC News Daily*, 3 February 2025.

23 "learning gap": Danielle Wood, "The jobs summit needs to think big: Here are 3 priorities for future-proofing Australia", *The Conversation*, 1 September 2022. For more detail, see Danielle Wood, "Inequality in Australia – what role does government policy play?", Hugh Stretton Oration, 22 May 2024.

23 Australians do not believe: Remy Varga, "Labor faces backlash over housing affordability crisis as concerns mount over falling standards of living", *The Daily Telegraph*, 14 October 2024.

25 "It's not accidental": Susan Neiman, *Left Is Not Woke*, Polity Press, 2023, p. 118.

25 "What it means": Anthony Albanese, *The Squiz*, 21 January 2025.

26 which means there are children starting school: Jane Caro, "The segregation crisis in schools funding", *The Saturday Paper*, 27 September 2025.

27 "a social democrat": Albanese, *Piers Morgan Uncensored*, YouTube, 3 May 2023.

27 "centrist": Jim Chalmers, quoted in "Politics with Michelle Grattan: An 'impatient' Jim Chalmers on taking political risks in Labor's second term", *The Conversation*, 18 June 2025.

27 "I think we're Labor": Anthony Albanese, quoted in Sean Kelly, "The year of living cautiously", *The Monthly*, June 2023.

28 a desire for the world to be a certain way: Here I draw on Adam Phillips, who writes "Indeed, we might think of Rorty's pragmatism as a kind of tribute to wishing; whenever we wish we are describing the life we want." (Adam Phillips, "On getting the life you want", *London Review of Books*, Vol. 46, No. 12, 20 June 2024.)

28 "fear of embarrassment": Neiman, *Left Is Not Woke*, p. 150.

28 blowing out candles: Adam Phillips raises this possibility in his work, for example asking, "What is the unconscious problem that your belief solves for you, or the wishes that it satisfies?" (Adam Phillips, "Freud's idols". *London Review of Books*, vol. 12, no. 18, 27 December 1990.)

29 "Absolutely": Albanese, quoted in Paul Karp, "Election 2022: Anthony Albanese backs 5.1% minimum wage rise to keep pace with inflation", *Guardian Australia*, 10 May 2022.

29 "is, by definition": John Searle, quoted in "John Searle obituary", *Guardian*, 5 October 2025.

29–30 "So what does he say": David Crowe, "'You can't simply wish things to happen': PM's message for progressives", *The Age/Sydney Morning Herald*, 20 May 2023.

30 a remarkable thing: the exact figure is 30 per cent, quoted by Cassandra Goldie in Michael Koziol, "No child will live in poverty? 30 years on, Bob Hawke's promise remains an elusive goal", *The Age/Sydney Morning Herald*, 13 June 2017.

30 reluctance to over-promise: Anthony Albanese, Radio 6PR, 26 May 2022.

32 "right up and down": Frank Bongiorno, "A New Australian Politics: Rupture or Realignment", UTS, 23 September 2025.

32 "This is about one thing": Jim Chalmers, Press conference, Logan, Queensland, 26 January 2024.

32 not frightening the horses: Kelly, "The year of living cautiously".

33 "we think": Anthony Albanese, Press conference, Sydney, 25 September 2025.

33 "grasp the nettle": Jim Chalmers, quoted in Michelle Grattan, "View from The Hill: Jim Chalmers wants to get on with economic reform and tax is in his sights", *The Conversation*, 18 June 2025.

33 "If you had a choice": Albanese, quoted in Greg Brown and Ben Packham, "Albanese faces union push for less work in return for productivity gains", *The Australian*, 20 July 2025.

34 "They seem to think": Don Watson, *Watsonia*, p. 37.

34 less monolithic, more dispersed, less unionised: this is a summary of a paragraph in Frank Bongiorno, "The continuing story of 'our' party", *Inside Story*, 10 November 2019.

34 in the 1960s: John Howard, Keynote speech, International Democratic Union Luncheon, Washington DC, 11 March 1996.

35 "Political scientists": Frank Bongiorno, "Whatever happened to Peter Dutton's would-be workers' party?", *Crikey*, 23 April 2025.

35 "It won't be a shortage": Jim Chalmers, "Address to the National Press Club: Economic reform in our second term", 18 June 2025.

35–6 "I'm in the crazy-brave category", etc.: Laurie Oakes, "It's fun. It's an adventure. It gets the adrenalin going", *Inside Story*, 21 September 2017.

36 "I fought it out": Michael Gordon, *A True Believer: Paul Keating*, University of Queensland Press, 1996 [1993], p. 127.

36 "I'm not in the consensus business": Paul Keating quoted in Elizabeth Farrelly, "Bad dreams of a front lawn for a 50-storey office park", *The Age/Sydney Morning Herald*, 5 February 2009.

36 "dust between", "Why": Peter Craven, "Paul Keating laments a rare musical talent", *The Australian*, 29 September 2019.

37 "it is now impossible": Mark Fisher, *Capitalist Realism: Is there no alternative?*, Zero Books, 2009.

38 "This is a miracle": Jonathan Haidt, quoted in Ezra Klein, "'Our kids are the least flourishing generation we know of'", *New York Times*, 1 April 2025.

38 "It's just bad": Klein, "Our kids are the least flourishing generation we know of".

38–9 "Today, the Australian people": Anthony Albanese, Election night speech, 3 May 2025.

39 "was that it meant": Chalmers, quoted in Paul Karp, "Jim Chalmers accuses Coalition of 'downward envy' as Dutton refuses to commit to JobSeeker increase in budget", *Guardian Australia*, 10 May 2023.

41 "Labour entered office", "the accusation": Malcolm Petrie, "When Labour was new", *London Review of Books*, 20 June 2024.

42 "Yet": Neville Wran, "Foreword", in McKinlay, *The ALP*, pp. v–vi.

43 Paul Kelly has written: Paul Kelly, *The End of Certainty: The story of the 1980s*, Allen & Unwin, 1992, p. 22.

43 "a new flag": Don Watson, *Recollections of a Bleeding Heart: A portrait of Paul Keating PM*, Anniversary Edition, Vintage Books, 2011, p. 848.

44 major parable: You can hear a version of both sides of this argument, for example, on "The 'reform-courage' spectrum", *Democracy Sausage with Mark Kenny*, 26 August 2025.

45 "I'm a Labor prime minister": Anthony Albanese, Q&A at the National Press Club, Canberra, 10 June 2025.

45 "in sync": Anthony Albanese quoted in Phillip Coorey, "No retreat on IR laws, Albanese tells business", *Australian Financial Review*, 17 September 2024.

46 "When a person": Richard Denniss, *Dead Centre: How political pragmatism is killing us*, Australia Institute Press, 2025, p. 109.

47 "It did not sound": Mike Steketee, "From messiah to mortal", *Inside Story*, 20 September 2022.

47 promoted globalisation and competition: For a comprehensive view of Labor's adoption of neoliberal policies, see Elizabeth Humphrys, *How Labour Built Neoliberalism: Australia's Accord, the Labour movement and the neoliberal project*, Brill, 2018.

47 too enamoured: Damien Murphy, "Labor's golden boy who transformed a nation", *The Age/Sydney Morning Herald*, 17 May 2019.

48 as Howard's attempts: For example, John Howard, "John Howard: Why bipartisanship is crucial to economic reform", *Australian Financial Review*, 17 August 2015.

48 another mistake in the years since: Jeff Sparrow touches on this argument in a review of Elizabeth Humphrys' book *Goodbye to All That: The End of Neoliberalism?*, *Sydney Review of Books*, 23 September 2019.

48 ferociously rejects: Tim Dunlop, "The path to neoliberalism", *The Future of Everything* blog, 6 August 2022, https://tdunlop.substack.com/p/the-path-to-neoliberalism, accessed 17 October 2025.

49 "not giving up gains": Albanese, *The Squiz*.

49 "We don't want": Anthony Albanese, "Strengthening Medicare", Launceston, 23 February 2025.

49 As others have noted: For example, Shaun Carney makes this point about the "Australian way" in "Albanese is the conservative who mugged the Liberals: Let's hope he seizes the moment", *The Age/Sydney Morning Herald*, 3 July 2025.

51 "progressive patriotism": Albanese, quoted in David Crowe and Paul Sakkal, "After three years, Albanese has a new slogan. Here's what 'progressive patriotism' means", *The Age/Sydney Morning Herald*, 15 May 2025.

52 "This is the most": Sean Kelly, *The Game: A portrait of Scott Morrison*, Black Inc., 2021, p. 250.

54 "On Saturday": Sean Kelly, "'Kind' Albanese seeks to reshape Australia in his image", *The Age/Sydney Morning Herald*, 5 May 2025.

55 "No, no": Anthony Albanese, Brisbane Drive, ABC Radio, 5 October 2023.

55 "My theory of governing": Jim Chalmers, quoted in Katharine Murphy, *Lone Wolf: Albanese and the new politics*, Quarterly Essay 88, November 2022, p. 87.

55 a book in defence of incrementalism: Greg Berman and Aubrey Fox, *Gradual: The case for incremental change in a radical age*, Oxford University Press, 2023. I reviewed Berman and Fox's book in "The incrementalists", *Inside Story*, 5 July 2023.

55 he told me in 2023: Anthony Albanese, quoted in Kelly, "The year of living cautiously".

55–6 "Paul said we gotta": Jennifer Hewett and Tony Boyd, "The lunch that changed Australia's economic destiny", *Australian Financial Review*, 6 September 2022.

56 "I had to essentially take on": Paul Keating, quoted in Tony Boyd, "Keating, Kelty share secrets to reform", *Australian Financial Review*, 6 September 2022.

56 "Virtually every": Kelly, *The End of Certainty*, p. 226.

56 "To look upon these programs": Raymond Moley, in a memoir, quoted in Alan Brinkley, *Franklin Delano Roosevelt*, Oxford University Press and the American Council of Learned Societies, 2010, p. 45.

56 "I'm petrified": Jim Chalmers, quoted in Deborah Snow, "'I don't do moderation, in anything': Why Treasurer Jim Chalmers went on the wagon", *The Age/Sydney Morning Herald*, 18 November 2023.

57 "Action, reaction": Anthony Albanese, quoted in Murphy, *Lone Wolf*, p. 39.

58 quality of "lightness": Katharine Murphy also refers to Albanese's "lightness": "This man can dance between raindrops." (Murphy, *Lone Wolf*, pp. 9–12)

58 Perseus succeeds: Italo Calvino, *Six Memos for the Next Millennium*, First Vintage International Edition, 1993, pp. 4–7.

58 "good people": Albanese, *Afternoon Briefing*, ABC TV, 1 September 2025.

59 Shaun Carney argues: Shaun Carney, "Albanese is ignoring Trump's demands – it will change our place in the world", *The Age/Sydney Morning Herald*, 14 August 2025.

60 "have any impact": Michele Bullock, quoted in Catie McLeod & Nick Visser, "Michele Bullock says 'nothing I can do personally' about house prices – as it happened", *Guardian Australia*, 30 September 2025.

60 "Year of Delivery": Albanese, quoted in Andrew Tillett, "Albanese vows 'year of delivery' as dominant Labor hits parliament", *Australian Financial Review*, 20 July 2025.

63 two halves to escape: I wrote about this in Sean Kelly, "Escape artists", *The Point*, 20 April 2020, https://thepointmag.com/quarantine-journal accessed 17 October 2025.

64 capitalism and democracy are diverging: Slobodian quoted in Daniel Immerwahr, "Zoning out", *The New York Review of Books*, 23 November 2023.

64 "They live in compounds": Immerwahr, "Zoning out".

64 "soft-secession": Quinn Slobodian, quoted in Gavin Jacobson, "Fantasies and fever dreams", *The New Statesman*, 15 April 2023.

64–5 T.J. Clark is correct: T.J. Clark, "For a left with no future", *New Left Review*, March/April 2012.

65–6 "upstream of all these trends": Putnam, quoted in Lulu Garcia-Navarro, "The Interview: Robert Putnam knows why you're lonely", *The New York Times*, 13 July 2024.

67 "the poet": Ben Lerner, *The Hatred of Poetry*, Fitzcarraldo Editions, 2016, p. 7.

68 "will always be about": Paul Keating, quoted in Gordon, *A True Believer*, p. 7.

68 lost futures: Mark Fisher writes at length on "lost futures" and their spectres in Mark Fisher, *Ghosts Of My Life: Writings on depression, hauntology and Lost Futures*, Zero Books, 2022.

69 "One should stress": Antonio Gramsci, *Prison Notebooks*, LeBooks Editora, 2024, p. 382.

69 "spirit of social democratic creativity": Anthony Albanese, John Curtin Oration, Sydney, 5 July 2025.

69 "Take a method": Franklin Roosevelt, quoted in Brinkley, *Franklin Delano Roosevelt*, p. 45.

69 "Instead of open conflict": Trevor Jackson, "'Never too much'", *The New York Review of Books*, 16 January 2025.

70 "It reads": Klein and Derek Thompson, *Abundance: How we build a better future*, Profile Books, 2025, p. 4.

72 Michel Serres: paraphrased in Adam Phillips, "On getting the life you want", *London Review of Books*, 20 June 2024.

73 "The great political leaders": Paul Keating, from transcript, *Mad About Music*, WQXR, 6 September 2009.

73 "writing is a cage", etc.: Elena Ferrante, translated by Ann Goldstein, *In the Margins: On the pleasures of reading and writing*, Europa Editions, 2022, pp. 73–81.

74 "cold surface", etc.: Elena Ferrante, quoted in "Elena Ferrante: The art of fiction No. 228", *Paris Review*, No. 212, Spring 2015.

Correspondence

Greg Bourne

In her Quarterly Essay, *Woodside vs the Planet*, Marian Wilkinson has exposed a sorry past and pointed to a bleak future. It is clear to me that the major oil and gas companies are banking on what the International Energy Agency's called the "Low International Co-operation Case." Sadly, you could surmise that the IEA has inadvertently signalled to the fossil-fuel companies that meaningful change is too hard – and that the only path forward is to obstruct net zero by 2050. For the oil and gas companies it's the "drill, baby, drill" world. It's "gas is our saviour transition fuel." It's "bank on building the silver bullet of carbon capture and storage (CCS)." Oh, and by the way, we have the technology, we just need lots of subsidies!

I have worked in the energy world since starting at the BP Kwinana refinery in Western Australia and have worked all over the world in oil, gas, LNG, wave power, photovoltaics and wind, and was for a time the executive in charge of BP's share in the North West Shelf (NWS) project. But since 1989 I have also been intimately involved in climate change mitigation planning and the world's need to transition swiftly away from fossil fuels and adapt our societies to rapidly changing climate conditions. Initially some of the companies, such as BP and Shell, embarked on the energy transition by getting out of coal and heavy oils, getting further into gas and investing in renewables. However, after twenty-five years of genuinely trying to morph into something different, many of these polluting companies have turned their backs on climate action.

Let's be clear, all fossil-fuel companies have been facing an existential crisis since climate change came on their radar like a squall on the horizon; they have been ducking and weaving ever since. But recently, two have been more open than most. In February 2025, BP's CEO, Murray Auchincloss, on announcing the new strategy to move away from renewable energy and concentrate on oil and gas, said, "Our optimism for a fast [energy] transition was misplaced, and we went too far, too fast." Then, in May, Woodside's Meg O'Neill told reporters at the post-announcement press conference of Woodside getting an extension to 2070 of its NWS gas plant, "We need to manage the pace of the energy transition, the renewables roll-out is not going as fast as had been initially anticipated." Laudable though their openness is, what they are not saying is that they, the oil and gas companies, need global and national climate talks to fail in order for their decades-long exploitation strategies to pay off. They also need their governments to be hooked on resource rents and taxes.

There is a Faustian bargain in play here. The governments sell their souls for some wealth in the present, while the devil, taking the largest cut, condemns the population to the tortures of hell – an overheating planet and how hellish it can be!

In the modelling and science of climate change there are many variables to consider. The Intergovernmental Panel on Climate Change uses integrated energy, economic and climate models to describe possible futures. These futures outline the degree of warming expected for various amounts of greenhouse gas emissions we emit globally. They also consider different ways we as a world might respond. In the "Sustainability" pathway, the world cooperates and swiftly reduces emissions to keep us below a 2°C rise in global temperature and preferably below a 1.5°C rise. We are not on that pathway – but there's still a narrow window of time to course-correct.

A pathway called "Regional Rivalry" (and energy insecurity) could well be the drum that is beating now, with current geopolitics in many parts of the world suggesting the world is seemingly willing to accept a rise of 3°C or greater. And it is in this world that the gas companies – particularly the LNG companies – place their faith, strategies and tactics. Play the devil, seduce and court the vanity and insecurity of politicians by promising short-term gains and discounting the long-term pain. Faust is hooked.

However, the pain we ordinary Australians face is plain for all to see in the recently released National Climate Risk Assessment. It groups findings under the headings "Changing Hazards," "Risks to People," "Risks to Places" and "Risks to Our Way of Life." It is a sobering and scary report but probably not of interest to current Woodside executives, who will be well gone by 2050. Those who follow and try to exploit gas reserves out to 2070 will find the north of Western Australia almost unworkable, such will be the heat stress.

The world of traded LNG is also likely to be highly volatile over the next few decades, leading to more short-term contracts and more difficult long-term contractual and financing arrangements – such will be the uncertainty of the future value of gas. "Promises" to the governments to cut climate pollution and undertake climate capture and storage will be found hollow and reneged upon. The liabilities for remediation and removal of ageing offshore plants and undersea pipelines will be passed back to governments as LNG companies exit. However, such is the allure of resource rents and taxes in the present that Faust will bargain once again – and the Australian people will lose.

Overall, the world is not decarbonising fast enough. The IEA quite rightly points out the myriad of decarbonisation opportunities in multiple sectors of the economy using numerous technologies. What is missing is the will. For the IEA, the key pillars of decarbonisation are energy efficiency, electrification, behavioural change, renewables, hydrogen and hydrogen-based fuels, bioenergy, and carbon capture, utilisation and storage. Within these pillars are opportunities ideal for any oil and gas company willing to embrace the future rather than hug the past. But that is not the case.

The leaders in the energy world today are investing in solar, wind, electric vehicles, batteries and grid technologies. They are looking at ways to electrify everything and decarbonise industrial processes. Capital is flowing in that direction and away from fossil fuels. Not only is China working on decarbonising its own economy, but by developing technologically advanced manufacturing industries it is also exporting the possibility to decarbonise to other countries – and reaping the economic benefits.

Australian LNG companies, Woodside in particular, only reluctantly reduce their domestic emissions but happily export their products and hope to do so until 2070. They push their products with the zeal of a drug lord: they do not care about the future misery they bring and the havoc they create; they care only about their dividends. Like drug lords, they brush aside resistance at the supply end of the chain and weaken the resolve of those at the demand end. They want their "customers" to remain hooked. Successive Australian governments are complicit in the trade – it has to stop.

Greg Bourne

WOODSIDE VS THE PLANET

Correspondence

Peter Garrett

Anyone trying to make sense of the gobsmacking contradictions in Australia's response to the rapidly escalating climate crisis – where policies ostensibly aimed at reducing greenhouse emissions starkly contrast with the continuing approval of massive gas developments likely to turbo-charge emissions – will find Marian Wilkinson's sober, excoriating analysis in *Woodside vs the Planet* both illuminating and infuriating. Illuminating, as Wilkinson exposes the bedrock character of fossil-fuel capitalism, tracking the trajectory of events, strategies and decisions leading to today's parallel universes, where despairing scientists and a concerned public grapple with the implications of a burning planet while a remorseless, determined fossil-fuel sector pushes on. Infuriating, as state capture – notably in Western Australia – is complete, regulatory processes are undermined, and ministers, premiers and resources-sector leaders all sing from the same focus-group-tested song sheet.

The Labor government in Canberra, despite the handsomest of majorities and extensive plans to reduce emissions and accelerate the transition to renewables, undercuts these good intentions by permitting the wholesale expansion of fossil-fuel schemes. Cabinet, understandably wringing its hands over calls on an ever-stretched federal budget, oversees the grossest tax inequity imaginable, while caucus and relevant committees are mute, the formerly progressive "Left" nowhere to be seen.

Marian Wilkinson's earlier book, *The Carbon Club*, and other examinations of the gas industry such as Royce Kurmelovs' *Pipeline to Power*, have ensured the modus operandi of the fossil-fuel sector is better understood. I hope policymakers and senior mandarins in Treasury and Finance will take note – all should be thankful for this in-depth exploration.

Woodside vs the Planet confirms that the fossil-fuel industry is a tax-avoiding, eco-cidal con job, whose activities impose great harm, a fact they have been fully aware of for decades. There is no evidence the two leading lights in Australia, Woodside and Santos, intend changing their ways. Indeed, the sector would have welcomed an LNP government win at the last election. Then literally all the regulatory shackles – modest as they were – would have been removed, with the North West Shelf project fast-tracked and Australia's greenhouse targets abandoned, as Peter Dutton proudly promised before sinking to a dismal defeat.

Further examination of the ideology of the fossil-fuel sector, characterised by underlying hostility and resistance to any government policy that impedes their business model as well as those who oppose their activities, is needed. Woodside CEO Meg O'Neill, who previously worked for Exxon, and a cast of executives, former ministers for resources, advisers and bureaucrats, inhabit a revolving-door ecosystem where downplaying climate change, relentless blocking of any meaningful attempts to regulate their activities and active denigration of environmental NGOs opposing the sector is accepted practice.

Hence O'Neill's unsurprising but revealing remarks about approvals "vulnerable to manipulation by activist groups whose only desire is to stop projects from proceeding." So much for young people's legitimate fear of what their lives might look like in a world hotter by 3°C.

A quick glance at the agenda and supporters of local right-wing groups, including the IPA and Advance Australia, and their importing of US-style rhetoric and campaign techniques, reveals an unrelenting hostility to government regulation or reform, which they view as "Soviet-style policy." Witness the degraded debate fuelled by these organisations in the Voice to Parliament referendum or current calls by conservative politicians to abandon net zero.

Woodside vs the Planet helps us better discern the political endpoint of continuing fossil-fuel exploitation, currently on full display in the United States, where expanding autocracy accompanies the reversal of positive climate action. Coal and gas companies are central to this destructive project, more than willing to desert democracy and sabotage efforts to maintain a safe planet while laughing all the way to the bank.

Barack Obama's observation – in 2014 – that "we are the first generation to feel the effects of climate change and the last generation who can do anything about it" brings home yet again, if this were needed, that we are in a crisis. Yet these words also convey the implicit message the fossil-fuel industry has promulgated over time, namely that "we" can all do something about a world that is overheating. Of course many within their limited spheres of influence do their best, but placing the onus on the individual lets leaders elected to protect the national interest and contain powerful forces who care little for the Commonwealth (in both meanings of the word), and the companies responsible for climate pollution, off the hook.

As activists, communities and Indigenous leaders continue to oppose the gas exploration and development cascading across northern Australia, often with little support from the more populated and prosperous south, and with state and federal governments in the gas industry's corner, the resilience of our polity is challenged.

Support those local communities and groups we must, while the government cannot approve twenty-seven new coal and gas export licences in its first term, nor sign off on the largest gas project in Australia's history, on the North West Shelf, and then expect to co-host the UN COP31 conference without the contradiction between its good intentions and reckless actions being highlighted far and wide.

As *Woodside vs the Planet* makes clear, our world and our way of life very much depend on leaders deciding in favour of a liveable planet. We are in a climate emergency and there is no time to lose.

Peter Garrett

WOODSIDE VS THE PLANET

Correspondence

Glen Gill

Unlike Marian Wilkinson, I am a retired professional engineer who has worked at very senior management levels in the electricity and gas industries in several countries, including over two decades in Australia. I have also been an adviser to many corporations and government agencies across Australia. I base my comments not on hearsay or on wild, uninformed statements from activists, but on science and extensive experience in the fossil-fuel and electricity industries.

My position is that this essay is a polemic, and its publication as a Quarterly Essay is based on Wilkinson's past reputation and not its content. First, I find the title, *Woodside vs the Planet*, ridiculous: the author is simply playing to the emotions of the uninformed masses, particularly the activists. It is difficult to understand that gas is not accepted as by far the preferred "fossil fuel," except in the transportation sector, and that its role is crucial as most OECD countries – except, of course, Australia – seek to wean themselves off coal and confine oil consumption mainly to the transportation sector.

The subtitle, *How a Company Captured a Country*, is equally misleading. Woodside, like all mining and petroleum companies operating in Australia, is a public company that "digs and delivers" resources owned by various governments pursuant to licences, regulations and permits issued by government bodies. As in all countries where the resources below ground are owned by the state, the state calls the shots, or should be calling the shots; the companies are merely agents working on behalf of and under the direction of the state. To say that such a company "captured the country" in which it operates is rather ridiculous. Blaming Woodside for any lack of proper resource stewardship by the owner of the resource is akin to blaming the driver of a vehicle for the atrocious condition of the Bruce Highway in Queensland. If Woodside were an Australian Commonwealth-owned company operating in Commonwealth-controlled ocean waters off Western Australia, then perhaps the subtitle would begin to make sense.

Wilkinson states that Woodside "is one of our biggest greenhouse polluters, not only at home but also globally." Of course, she does not provide a shred of evidence to support this claim. Wood Mackenzie, a globally accepted expert in this field, reported the following findings in February 2025: "Gas produces only half the carbon dioxide of coal and 70% of oil when burned, and generates considerably less pollution, making it the cleanest fossil fuel option. Replacing coal with natural gas has already helped deliver substantial CO_2 reduction and can help decarbonize markets across Asia which remain dependent on coal. Gas-fired plants are key to providing reliable and flexible supply supporting the integration of intermittent renewable energy sources. Natural gas can act as a catalyst for advancing other lower-carbon technologies, including carbon capture and storage (CCS) and low-carbon hydrogen."

To state that Woodside is responsible for any emissions or leaks of gas associated with its LNG exports to Japan, China and Korea is wildly misleading. It assumes that if Woodside did not produce and sell LNG, then these countries would go without! Although Australia has become the world's second-largest LNG exporter behind the United States, supplying 19.7 per cent of the global LNG trade in 2025, it is only the seventh-largest gas producer worldwide. Its total production accounts for less than 4 per cent of global gas (the vast majority of which is pipeline gas, not LNG). Japan, China and Korea can source LNG from several other countries and will easily do so if Woodside does not produce LNG.

To describe the Woodside assets on the North West Shelf as a "carbon bomb" and therefore a detriment to the global environment is nothing but useless and extreme activist language. Activists don't debate or make written arguments, they simply protest and broadcast a narrative of fear, ignorance and hatred. Ironically, the organic-loving activists apparently didn't study organic chemistry, and they are oblivious to the petrochemical industry, which uses gas as the main feedstock.

Australia lets other countries do the hard lifting as it elects to export LNG rather than add value to its gas resources, and then complains about the carbon footprint associated with value-adding in the form of converting a gas into a liquid for transportation purposes. Other gas-rich OECD countries, such as Canada and the United States, must make the plastics, fertilisers, explosives, etc., using their own gas feedstocks while making a carbon footprint in doing so, as do all industrial activities, and then export the finished products to Australia! I can't begin to accept such duplicity.

Glen Gill

WOODSIDE VS THE PLANET

Correspondence

David Ritter

As a West Australian by origin, I'm always a bit apprehensive about how someone from the outside – an "eastern stateser," as we like to say – will perceive and write about the place. I needn't have been concerned about Marian Wilkinson, because she's done a fine job of evoking the dark compromise of Western Australia's political economy with acuity but without condescension. The "Western Third" has always been a contested place, where a certain innate conservatism has found expression in both extractivist and conservationist impulses, which exist in deep tension with one another. Wilkinson has richly evoked this discordance, which underlies the epic dispute that now surrounds Woodside Energy and its plans to industrialise the waters surrounding Australia's largest oceanic reef system, the paradisiacal Scott Reef, to keep processing gas until 2070.

If Wilkinson's framing is to be accepted and Woodside has "captured a country," then, as with every occupation, there is a growing popular insurgency. The scale of the public resistance to the plans of the fossil-fuel giant is a key element of the story. Wilkinson mentions in her essay that Greenpeace handed over a 440,000-strong petition calling on the then federal environment minister, Tanya Plibersek, to stop Woodside's destructive gas expansion plans. When initially presented, that entreaty was already understood to be one of the largest in Australian parliamentary history. When resubmitted a year later to the new minister, Senator Murray Watt, the number of signatories had swelled to almost 550,000.

The ubiquity of Woodside's brand, as described by Wilkinson – spread across sport, community and cultural institutions, as well as Perth's business skyline – nourishes rather than stifles an underlying restlessness about the power of the company. There is disquiet across various fronts, among which the threat Woodside's activities pose to Western Australia's oceans is becoming increasingly difficult to ignore. The love for those magnificent waves that break on the west coast, and the miraculous creatures that live within them, is a non-negotiable part of Western

Australia's shared identity. The petrochemical industry, of which Woodside is one of the most prominent examples in the state, is a mortal threat to the flourishing of the marine environment that West Australians love and of which we are proud: our clean oceans are indeed the envy of the world. Snorkelling, surfing, ocean swimming and whale-watching are practically considered our birthright.

Wilkinson is not the first Quarterly Essayist to have set out the reality that Australia's national environmental protection laws, contained in the *Environmental Protection and Biodiversity Conservation Act* and associated legislation, are not fit for purpose. More than a decade ago, Tim Flannery reflected on the failure of our laws to halt extinctions. Despite some iconic successes, Australia's overall inability to protect and nurture our national natural estate has become notorious as a failure of public policy. Multiple reviews, including those by the late Allan Hawke, and more recently by Professor Graeme Samuel, have elaborated in detail why the current system and its decision-makers have not prevented dire ecological decline across our continent. After the notorious failed attempt in its first term, the re-elected Albanese government has pledged to try again with a reform package, and an intensive process is now underway, in which I am deeply engaged. At the time of writing, things remain fluid and the opportunity is there to secure meaningful improvements on redline issues, including addressing Australia's chronic deforestation levels and bringing climate change more squarely under the aegis of the EPBC *Act*. This should not be so hard. Wise ecological stewardship should be non-negotiable for every government. As bizarre as it may be to have to be explicit about this, our national environmental protection laws should be effective in protecting the environment.

Setting the outcome of the current reform process to one side, if ever there was something that can and should be protected under the EPBC *Act* as it stands, it's the ecological treasure that is Scott Reef. As I noted to Marian Wilkinson in my interview for her essay, there is a clear opportunity for the environment minister simply to say "no" to Woodside's Browse project under existing nature protection laws because of the unique environmental value of Scott Reef. It is worth setting out this pathway in greater detail.

When making decisions under the EPBC *Act*, the minister must consider the potential for projects such as Woodside's Browse to have a significant impact on threatened species or ecological communities. There is also an additional safeguard for all cetaceans (whales, dolphins and porpoises) in Australian waters. Key factors that are considered include the nature of the potential impact (intensity, duration, magnitude, geographic extent), the sensitivity of the site, the value and quality of the affected environment, and the effectiveness of any avoidance or mitigation measures.

Scott Reef is an astonishing place that is still in remarkable condition despite the rising threats to our oceans. By virtue of its splendid isolation, it is a haven for a broad range of marine species, many of which are protected under the *EPBC Act*. While the nearby Rowley Shoals suffered 90 per cent impacts from coral bleaching, reports are now coming through that Scott Reef has survived relatively unscathed. Those fortunate few who have visited this remote, incredible marine wonderworld are awe-struck by what they have seen. At least twelve species of dolphin have been sighted at the reef, along with ten separate kinds of whale. The endangered pygmy blue whale migrates through Scott Reef as a vital feeding place, and the reef supports the largest known population of the endangered dusky sea snake. A genetically distinct community of threatened green turtles return to Scott Reef and Browse Island to breed. The risks to all this from Woodside's plans are very direct. Sandy Islet, where the green turtles lay their eggs, could literally vanish from a combination of subsidence and rising sea levels, for example. Damage from the extensive seismic blasting that Woodside wants to undertake could injure whales' hearing and drive them out of critical habitat.

The minister may also consider various other matters, including the environmental record of the proponent. Woodside's record includes an oil spill earlier this year, a whale calf collision, and delays in the removal of large-scale pieces of disused fossil-fuel infrastructure. On the latter, Woodside was ordered four times over four years by the offshore regulator, NOPSEMA, to decommission large-scale infrastructure used in its Nganhurra operations, including the Nganhurra Riser Turret Mooring, which was falling apart just 19 kilometres from the Ningaloo Coast UNESCO World Heritage Property. In May 2023, Greenpeace sailed the *Rainbow Warrior* to the Riser Turret and activists hung a giant banner off the massive piece of decaying junk which read "WOODSIDE, DON'T BE A TOSSER." Five months later, Woodside issued a media statement saying the structure had been removed.

It is obvious that the environment minister, Murray Watt, should do what he can to protect Scott Reef: if not this vital ecological paradise, then where? But no ministerial decision is ever a foregone conclusion, not least in this case, for all the reasons that Marian Wilkinson documents in her essay. Yet for both state and federal Labor, Scott Reef is a genuine legacy question. Protecting Australia's largest oceanic reef system would be right up there with the ALP's part in saving the Daintree Rainforest, the Franklin River and Antarctica, and the introduction of the first Great Barrier Reef Marine Park Bill to the federal parliament in May 1975.

The Albanese government was re-elected with a massive mandate, partly on the strength of the Australian electorate's visceral reaction to the spectacle of what a second Trump presidency was unleashing on the United States. Woodside's connections to the Trumpian project had not been widely commented upon, and it's timely and important that Wilkinson has brought to light the significance of Trump's re-election in emboldening Woodside's aggressive expansion plans. After the publication of Wilkinson's essay, Woodside CEO Meg O'Neill stood with Trump ally and MAGA Republican stalwart Louisiana Governor Jeff Landry to "break ground" on Woodside's planned new US$17.5-billion production and export facility in Calcasieu Parish of that state. Photographs showed O'Neill, Landry and others holding shovels beneath a vast banner of the Stars and Stripes. Woodside included effusive praise from Trump-aligned US politicians in its media release about the gala day. Trump's Secretary of the Interior – oil man and climate denier Doug Burgum – called the ground-breaking "another win for President Trump's American Energy Dominance Agenda."

O'Neill has previously said that Australia "loses on every front" to the US, including on environmental and labour grounds. "Australia must sharpen its competitive advantage," she has lectured us. Perhaps she thinks Australians are a bunch of losers because we prefer fairer wages, stronger environmental protections and more progressive taxation and we don't want our oceans destroyed by the gas industry she champions. So be it. But I can promise Meg O'Neill that the fossil-fuel energy domination agenda pursued by Woodside and its pals in the White House will continue to be resisted until common sense prevails. The people of Western Australia – and Australia as a whole – don't want Woodside, or Trump, or anyone else, ruining our oceans and our future.

David Ritter

WOODSIDE VS THE PLANET

Correspondence

Felicity Deane

Marian Wilkinson's Quarterly Essay reveals a central challenge in Australian governance: the enduring influence of vested industry power on political decision-making. Through her case study of Woodside Energy, Wilkinson exposes the government's vulnerability and demonstrates that, despite increasingly urgent environmental concerns, its capacity to act decisively is consistently compromised when doing so requires confronting powerful corporate interests.

Australia's current political landscape exacerbates this problem. The Opposition, whose role is to hold the government accountable and prioritise public interests, has become just another contender in securing industry backing. Not to mention its position on climate change, which can only be described as scientifically irresponsible. The result is a decade of political game-playing and poor leadership hindering meaningful climate policy. While Australia has a small population, the resource-rich landscape of the nation means that when Scope 1, 2 and 3 emissions are considered, Australia's greenhouse gas emissions are among the highest in the world.

The challenge posed by fossil-fuel interests is not only an Australian problem but a global one. Australia's political economy matters profoundly to the international climate response, given the scale of emissions linked to its fossil-fuel exports and associated Scope 3 emissions. However, the Australian public is too often encouraged to conflate the success of these companies with the national interest, despite the reality that profits derived from sovereign resources provide little recompense to the public and primarily enrich shareholders and senior executives.

In his submission to the Economic Reform Roundtable, Ross Garnaut observed that "real wages and living standards hardly grew at all in the nine years from 2013 until the election of the Albanese Labor Government in 2022." This raises an important question: if the mining industry is promoted as essential to Australia's prosperity, why have the substantial profits of a few resource companies failed to translate into broader benefits for middle-class Australians, even though these resources are sovereign assets? Instead, this justification serves as a smokescreen to allow pursuit of corporate interests and the erosion of already weak environmental protections. The Australian public has been the subject of government gaslighting (pun intended), with politicians claiming that the natural gas industry is indispensable for the low-carbon energy transition. This propaganda is uncovered in the essay where Wilkinson highlights that gas delivers only around 25 per cent fewer emissions than coal. Hardly the panacea for a nation on track to fall well short of agreed international targets. However, alternative pathways will not be explored due to the power wielded by corporations such as Woodside.

This power (which ultimately leads to a form of government corruption) derives in part from the significant time and resources major corporations devote to cultivating close relationships with those in parliamentary positions. The capacity of large corporations to influence law and policy is fundamentally tied to their lobbying power and the scale of their financial investments. In Australia, where restrictions on political donations are minimal and only contributions above $17,300 must be disclosed, the full extent to which corporate spending translates into political persuasion is often obscured. In the past two years, two private member's bills have sought to improve transparency around federal lobbying, but their prospects of becoming law remain slim despite their importance for good governance. While Australia does regulate lobbyists through the federal Lobbying Code of Conduct, its reach is limited to third-party, "professional" lobbyists acting for clients. It excludes businesses and industry associations lobbying government directly, whether through executives or in-house lobbyists. This regulatory gap is a crucial element in understanding the persistent weaknesses of Australia's climate-change mitigation policies (among other regulatory shortcomings).

Unfortunately, these compounding circumstances have meant that the regulatory responses to climate change ever since the Carbon Pricing Mechanism was repealed have been riddled with half-measures, errors and ill-conceived responses. Since 2014, the Australian response has effectively gamed the international obligation to achieve genuine emissions reductions. Poor political behaviour and problematic ideology have delayed action and we have lost more than ten important years in the race to keep warming below 2°C (although blame must be shared with many nations around the world). Further, the *perception* of doing something, which is what the Safeguard Mechanism does, may be worse than doing nothing at all.

The Safeguard Mechanism has been described by some as a carbon price. It is not. Instead, it operates as a baseline-and-credit scheme, applying to just 219 facilities nationwide, considerably fewer than the almost 400 covered under the Gillard government's Carbon Pricing Mechanism (which actually *was* a carbon price).

Under the Safeguard Mechanism, facilities incur no cost so long as their emissions remain below an allocated baseline; only when they exceed it must they purchase credits, while reductions achieved below the baseline can generate tradable credits for future compliance. Although baselines are intended to decline gradually, they are unlikely to impose a meaningful carbon price before 2050, when net zero is expected. In practice, the scheme functions primarily as a framework for offsets, which currently must be met with Australian Carbon Credit Units. Should international offsets be permitted, the mechanism will collapse from being an offset scheme into a form of climate deception.

Wilkinson's essay also signals a deeper dilemma: the inherent difficulty of accounting for greenhouse gas emissions. To explain, Scope 3 emissions from Australia's fossil-fuel exports are not included in the national greenhouse gas inventory. In accordance with UN reporting guidelines, emissions are accounted for on a production basis, meaning they are attributed to the country where the fuels are combusted rather than the country of extraction. Therefore, the international means for allocating emissions to a particular jurisdiction ensures that only direct Scope 1 emissions are included in any national total (which is not something the Australian government alone can correct). This approach avoids double-counting across parties to international agreements, but at the same time means that production-based inventories do not fully reflect the climate implications of fossil-fuel export economies and vice versa. One could argue that there are important reasons for only counting emissions once in the global total; however, we should recognise that the law and policy within a given jurisdiction can have a direct effect on the availability of fossil fuels in another. The disconnect that supports a nation to extract fossil fuels without any responsibility for their emissions is one of the reasons that fossil fuels remain an affordable form of energy production. However, again, it is not the accounting that needs to shift, it is the initial approval for projects.

Hence, the answer is not necessarily to include Scope 3 emissions in each nation's inventories. To do so would ultimately result in double counting. This would render the inventory process even more meaningless in terms of allocating accountability for failed climate policies. Alternatively, if, instead of double counting, responsibility for fossil-fuel emissions was allocated to the extracting nation, there would be mixed results based on the climate mitigation policies that existed within that jurisdiction. For instance, if Australia was deemed responsible for exported fossil-fuel emissions but was without a robust carbon price, those externalities would still be largely overlooked. In contrast to this, when fossil fuels are combusted in jurisdictions with a carbon price, their use is more likely to (at least partially) reflect the true economic costs of their use. As a result, one could argue that allocating emissions to nations with a carbon price is better for the planet. In these jurisdictions, energy generated from fossil fuels will become less competitive and be the subject of reduced demand.

Accordingly, the ability to address the carbon bomb that is the North West Shelf does not require international negotiations to modify responsibility for Scope 3 emissions (thankfully, because this avenue is unlikely to lead to easy solutions). Instead, as Albanese proposed in 2005, the minister must be forced to consider the greenhouse gas emissions that will result from any project approval through a climate trigger under the *Environment Protection and Biodiversity Conservation Act*. Once activated, such a trigger should address, or at least recognise, Scope 3 emissions without requiring a wholesale shift in the international emissions accounting regime. That is, of course, if the minister exercises discretion appropriately.

Felicity Deane

WOODSIDE VS THE PLANET

Correspondence

Shaun Watson & Kate Wylie

Marian Wilkinson's "elephant in the room" is big, powerful and greedy. It is emblazoned with the Woodside logo and drags the two major parties along behind it. Doctors for the Environmental Australia (DEA) knows this elephant well, having recently met it at close quarters in the Federal Court in our case against the National Offshore Petroleum Safety and Environmental Management Authority (NOPSEMA) and Woodside.

As doctors, we consider it our duty of care to reduce the health impacts of climate change in any way that is guided by evidence. We pursued a chink in the elephant's armour regarding the government regulator NOPSEMA's approval of Woodside's environmental plan for the Scarborough offshore gas project. With the support of the Environment Defenders Office, we disputed the approval through a judicial review. The essence of our argument was that Woodside did not adequately define a minimally acceptable risk to the environment from the Scope 3 greenhouse gas emissions produced by Scarborough operations and that NOPSEMA therefore should not have approved its environmental plan.

We brought our case to court in the public interest. Climate change is driven by greenhouse gas emissions and is a severe threat to public health. We are treating the impacts of climate pollution, extreme heat and severe weather in our practices and hospitals now and know that the burden of disease will continue to grow as our planet continues to heat. We hold grave concerns about the approval of any project that causes greenhouse gas emissions, because all these emissions combine to cause harm. Woodside's environmental plan argues that the staggering 878 million tonnes of CO_2 planned to be produced by Scarborough across its projected life are "de minimis," or of negligible environmental impact. For doctors, just as every cigarette does damage, every tonne of carbon dioxide equivalent adds to global heating and health harms.

The court rejected our challenge, upholding NOPSEMA's approval of Woodside's environmental plan. However, this decision rested on the regulatory processes, not on a lack of understanding or acceptance of climate science, as evidenced by Justice McElwaine's statement: "It is not for this Court to adjudicate on the existential threat posed by climate change caused by anthropogenic CO2 emissions to the atmosphere."

Further, there were several important tactical victories along the way. The court granted us standing, despite vigorous opposition from Woodside. In this context, standing means that Doctors for the Environment Australia had the right to make the challenge, by virtue of its legitimate concern for the health impacts of climate change. This is no small victory and serves as a precedent for other non-government organisations in similar circumstances. More specifically, it suggests that we can remain in the game of scrutinising the execution of this project and further environmental plans. It is particularly noteworthy that Justice McElwaine made clear that NOPSEMA has the power to revoke the environmental plan if Woodside does not live up to its commitments, including those regarding Scope 3 greenhouse gas emissions – that is, those resulting from the consumption of the gas it exports overseas.

We were granted a protective cost order based on the recognition that our appeal was reasonable, in the public interest and would not be able to proceed if we faced the existential threat of full costs in the event of defeat. The order also allowed us to raise funds to cover costs, again setting a precedent for others to follow.

Most strikingly, the case has clarified Woodside's approach to gas exports, referred to in submissions as the displacement assumption. The gas from Scarborough is purported to "have an ongoing role in supporting customers' plans to secure their energy needs, while they reduce their emissions" and has a role to play in reducing dependence on carbon-intensive fuels. A curious line of reasoning in our opinion, considering the gas is methane, a greenhouse gas with eighty times the intensity of CO_2 over twenty years. For us, this is akin to saying vaping reduces health harms by displacing cigarettes.

To sit in the front row while the barristers soliloquised and the judge considered evidence was fascinating and enervating in equal measure. Those of us who see clearly the elephant in the room must continue to work with all the tools at our disposal, including the legal system. We at Doctors for the Environment Australia emerged from this legal battle with admiration for the intelligence, capacity and tenacity of our legal colleagues, but also with a sober awareness of the limits to the Federal Court's appetite for activism and its tendency to support business as usual. Our advice is to approach any future challenge with courage tempered by careful deliberation and preparation and ensure that risks are mitigated through a protective cost order. Not only does such an order avoid financial catastrophe, it implies that the court has some sympathy for your organisation and arguments and considers that running the case is in the public interest. It is a way of testing the water, rather than jumping in the deep end.

Fundamentally, the courts work within the scope of the law. If "the elephant" is the fossil-fuel industry, then "the room" is the political sphere where laws are made. Wilkinson paints a grim picture of our current state capture, but even this is not unalterable. Working together, we can rescind the social licence of the fossil-fuel industry, focusing on the hazardous health impacts of coal, oil and gas. The political licence will follow once our elected representatives realise that electoral pain lies down the path of business as usual.

Shaun Watson & Kate Wylie

WOODSIDE VS THE PLANET

Response to Correspondence

Marian Wilkinson

It was clear to me writing this essay that despite the Paris Agreement, the gulf in thinking between the fossil-fuel industry and the climate movement in Australia is as wide as ever. As a journalist, I see this gulf reflected daily in the mainstream media, where business reporters by and large write about gas and coal projects through the lens of profitability, jobs and the CEO's vision, with little reference to climate science except for a pro forma nod to net zero. In the same publications, the environment reporter, in isolation, will write about the latest dire warning from a leading scientist on the closing window of opportunity to hold global warming below 2°C. Too often, these stories never intersect.

One of my aims with *Woodside vs the Planet* was to bridge this gulf in thinking and raise the need for a wider national debate on Australia's role as a world-leading fossil-fuel exporter in the age of climate change. For me, the Woodside story embodies this nation's dilemma. Its ambitious Burrup Hub developments, and its plans to run the giant North West Shelf gas plant to 2070 by drilling new wells in the Browse Basin, have sparked ferocious opposition from Australia's climate movement. But there has been limited political debate about the long-term viability of this gas growth strategy in the business media or in parliaments, state and federal.

The debate over Woodside's plans is not just about climate change and its impacts, vital as this is; it is also about whether Australia will prosper in the global energy transition. Australia's decades-long commitment to its fossil-fuel export business, and to Woodside in particular, is entrenched in state and federal policy-making. Since Paris, politicians on both sides have supported the gas industry's claim that our LNG exports are critical to supporting the energy transition and helping Asia to decarbonise even as global emissions keep rising and global investment in renewables keeps growing. Given so much is at stake in these decarbonisation claims, they need to be tested in our parliaments and in the federal bureaucracy.

The responses to the essay provide some very important contributions to this debate, as well as reflecting the gulf between the two sides. Peter Garrett has the advantage of speaking both as a former Labor environment minister who saw this policy-making from the inside and as a passionate conservationist. He accurately describes today's "parallel universes" of despairing scientists and a determined fossil-fuel sector that keeps pushing on. Garrett channels the frustration and anger of many climate veterans I spoke to, and of many ordinary voters, alarmed by the Albanese government's continued support for large coal and gas export projects despite the urgent warnings of climate scientists.

His alarm is clearly shared by David Ritter from Greenpeace and Shaun Watson and Kate Wylie from Doctors for the Environment Australia. DEA are one of several non-government organisations that have attempted to stymie Woodside's Burrup Hub developments in court. Their case raised the thorny issue of the impact of Woodside's Scope 3 emissions, the emissions produced by customers burning Woodside's exported gas in Asia. Significantly, Watson and Wylie report how their experience brought home the limits of the Federal Court's appetite for climate cases around Scope 3 emissions and who bears the responsibility for them. Until recently, it was widely accepted that, under the UN framework on climate change, responsibility lay with the customers, not the fossil-fuel companies or countries profiting from the exports.

This is where Professor Felicity Deane's response is helpful. As she rightly explains, Scope 3 emissions are not included in Australia's national greenhouse inventory under the UN rules to avoid the issue of "double counting" between producers and customers whose countries are parties to climate treaties. The trouble is, this disconnect favours fossil-fuel-producing nations that license companies to extract and export gas and coal without taking responsibility for the emissions shipped offshore. Unless the customer's home country imposes a robust carbon price, the customer has limited incentive to switch to cleaner energy, even in those countries with national emissions reduction targets.

Deane's response lends support to climate lawyers who argue that the reform of our national environment laws, the *EPBC Act*, needs to include climate considerations – a "climate trigger." This would require approvals for big fossil-fuel projects to address their Scope 3 emissions and their potential climate impact, along with any carbon price in the customer country. This would avoid the need to upend international emissions accounting under the UN framework but spread the responsibility for fossil-fuel emissions across exporters and importers and incentivise the shift to cleaner energy.

A climate trigger is arguably even more important for the Albanese government to consider today, given the recent advisory opinion of the International Court of

Justice. That unanimous opinion found the responsibility of fossil-fuel-producing countries for greenhouse gas emissions under international law is not limited to UN climate agreements and could leave producers and the governments that license them open to claims for damages and reparations from those suffering the impacts of climate change. But it looks unlikely that climate change will be in the frame in the government's EPBC reforms right now, given the hostility of coal and gas producers, including Woodside, to a climate trigger – unless the Opposition refuses to play ball and Environment Minister Murray Watt is forced to negotiate with the Greens in the Senate.

The divisions between the gas industry and the climate movement on the responsibility for Scope 3 emissions are starkly set out in the contributions of Glen Gill and Greg Bourne, both of whom worked in the gas industry. Gill mounts a staunch defence of the industry's decarbonisation claims and rails against what he sees as the narrative of "fear, ignorance and hatred" coming from climate activists, in contrast to his own views, which, he says, are based on his extensive industry experience and "on science." But alas not on climate science, which is what will determine whether global warming is contained to 1.5°C or soars over 3°C.

Greg Bourne, who once played a role in the North West Shelf project for UK gas giant BP, believes the strategies of the global gas companies, including Woodside, are more aligned with a 3°C temperature rise. And this explains why the uproar in the climate movement over Woodside's plans is not going away anytime soon. In the months since the essay was published, the big environment groups have doubled down on the fight over the Burrup Hub. The Australian Conservation Foundation has launched a new legal challenge to the NWS extension on the grounds that Watt failed to properly consider its climate change impacts.

There is another important update on my essay about Woodside's Burrup plans – their impact on Indigenous heritage, the World Heritage–listed Murujuga rock art. At the time of publication, Watt had conditionally approved the NWS extension but stressed that this approval included "strict conditions" to protect the rock art from Woodside's industrial emissions, as opposed to its greenhouse emissions. Those conditions were not released until after publication, and after much wrangling between Watt and Woodside, which saw the conditions watered down when Woodside said it could not accept them. In the end, Watt judged that the economic importance of Woodside's gas plans outweighed his department's original idea to push Woodside to cut the most polluting industrial emissions below detectable air emissions. Woodside argued this was not technically feasible and would amount to an "effective refusal" of the extension of the NWS gas plant – which of course would have provoked a political crisis in Western Australia and Canberra.

I urge anyone interested to read the department's full advice and Watt's response to see how the approval finally got up. It's seventy-four pages of extraordinary policy gymnastics and it's all up on the department's website. It gives Joseph Heller's *Catch-22* a run for its money. Buried in there are Watt and his department's doubts over claims by the WA Murujuga Rock Art Monitoring Program (MRAMP) this year that the "most likely" cause of the damage detected on the rocks on the Burrup was historical industrial emissions, not current ones. This claim was repeated by WA premier Roger Cook but was fiercely contested at the time by UWA's Professor Ben Smith. The final approval reveals that Watt agreed with his department that "there is considerable uncertainty about the MRAMP hypothesis that impacts were caused by historical emissions given the numerous existing and proposed emissions sources." He noted, as did my essay, that the biggest source of industrial emissions pollution on the Burrup today is Woodside's Karratha gas plant, the heart of the North West Shelf project. He also agreed with his department that, over the lifetime of the project out to 2070, the industrial emissions could cause degradation and damage to the rock art. Despite this, Watt decided on a slower timetable for Woodside to progressively cut its industrial emissions – meaning some would still be detectable out past 2060. The impact on the rock art, he judged, would be small, outweighed by the economic and social benefits from Woodside's project.

Marian Wilkinson

Greg Bourne is currently a Climate Councillor and has been regional president of BP Australasia, CEO of WWF Australia and chair of the Australian Renewable Energy Agency.

Felicity Deane is an associate professor at the Queensland University of Technology.

Peter Garrett is a former cabinet minister in the Rudd/Gillard governments and long-time conservation activist and musician with Midnight Oil.

Glen Gill has over forty years of global experience in the petroleum and electricity industries, including in technical, commercial, regulatory and public policy areas.

Sean Kelly is the author of *The Game: A portrait of Scott Morrison*, a columnist for the Nine newspapers and regular contributor to *The Monthly*, and a former adviser to Labor prime ministers.

David Ritter is CEO of Greenpeace Australia Pacific.

Shaun Watson is a Sydney-based neurologist and chair of the NSW Committee of Doctors for the Environment Australia.

Marian Wilkinson is a multi-award-winning investigative journalist. Her books include *The Fixer*, *Dark Victory* (with David Marr) and *The Carbon Club*.

Kate Wylie is a GP and executive director of Doctors for the Environment Australia.

QUARTERLY ESSAY BACK ISSUES

- ☐ **QE 1** *In Denial* by Robert Manne $27.99
- ☐ **QE 2** *Appeasing Jakarta* by John Birmingham $27.99
- ☐ **QE 3** *The Opportunist* by Guy Rundle $27.99
- ☐ **QE 4** *Rabbit Syndrome* by Don Watson $27.99
- ☐ **QE 5** *Girt By Sea* by Mungo MacCallum $27.99
- ☐ **QE 6** *Beyond Belief* by John Button $27.99
- ☐ **QE 7** *Paradise Betrayed* by John Martinkus $27.99
- **QE 8** *Groundswell* by Amanda Lohrey OUT OF STOCK
- ☐ **QE 9** *Beautiful Lies* by Tim Flannery $27.99
- ☐ **QE 10** *Bad Company* by Gideon Haigh $27.99
- ☐ **QE 11** *Whitefella Jump Up* by Germaine Greer $27.99
- ☐ **QE 12** *Made in England* by David Malouf $27.99
- ☐ **QE 13** *Sending Them Home* by Robert Manne with David Corlett $27.99
- ☐ **QE 14** *Mission Impossible* by Paul McGeough $27.99
- ☐ **QE 15** *Latham's World* by Margaret Simons $27.99
- ☐ **QE 16** *Breach of Trust* by Raimond Gaita $27.99
- ☐ **QE 17** *'Kangaroo Court'* by John Hirst $27.99
- ☐ **QE 18** *The Worried Well* by Gail Bell $27.99
- ☐ **QE 19** *Relaxed & Comfortable* by Judith Brett $27.99
- ☐ **QE 20** *A Time for War* by John Birmingham $27.99
- ☐ **QE 21** *What's Left? by Clive Hamilton* $27.99
- ☐ **QE 22** *Voting for Jesus* by Amanda Lohrey $27.99
- ☐ **QE 23** *The History Question* by Inga Clendinnen $27.99
- ☐ **QE 24** *No Fixed Address* by Robyn Davidson $27.99
- ☐ **QE 25** *Bipolar Nation* by Peter Hartcher $27.99
- ☐ **QE 26** *His Master's Voice* by David Marr $27.99
- ☐ **QE 27** *Reaction Time* by Ian Lowe $27.99
- ☐ **QE 28** *Exit Right* by Judith Brett $27.99
- ☐ **QE 29** *Love & Money* by Anne Manne $27.99
- ☐ **QE 30** *Last Drinks* by Paul Toohey $27.99
- ☐ **QE 31** *Now or Never* by Tim Flannery $27.99
- ☐ **QE 32** *American Revolution* by Kate Jennings $27.99
- ☐ **QE 33** *Quarry Vision* by Guy Pearse $27.99
- ☐ **QE 34** *Stop at Nothing* by Annabel Crabb $27.99
- ☐ **QE 35** *Radical Hope* by Noel Pearson $27.99
- ☐ **QE 36** *Australian Story* by Mungo MacCallum $27.99
- ☐ **QE 37** *What's Right?* by Waleed Aly $27.99
- ☐ **QE 38** *Power Trip* by David Marr $27.99
- ☐ **QE 39** *Power Shift* by Hugh White $27.99
- ☐ **QE 40** *Trivial Pursuit* by George Megalogenis $27.99
- ☐ **QE 41** *The Happy Life* by David Malouf $27.99
- ☐ **QE 42** *Fair Share* by Judith Brett $27.99
- ☐ **QE 43** *Bad News* by Robert Manne $27.99
- ☐ **QE 44** *Man-Made World* by Andrew Charlton $27.99
- ☐ **QE 45** *Us and Them* by Anna Krien $27.99
- ☐ **QE 46** *Great Expectations* by Laura Tingle $27.99
- ☐ **QE 47** *Political Animal* by David Marr $27.99
- ☐ **QE 48** *After the Future* by Tim Flannery $27.99
- ☐ **QE 49** *Not Dead Yet* by Mark Latham $27.99
- ☐ **QE 50** *Unfinished Business* by Anna Goldsworthy $27.99
- ☐ **QE 51** *The Prince* by David Marr $27.99
- ☐ **QE 52** *Found in Translation* by Linda Jaivin $27.99
- ☐ **QE 53** *That Sinking Feeling* by Paul Toohey $27.99
- ☐ **QE 54** *Dragon's Tail* by Andrew Charlton $27.99
- ☐ **QE 55** *A Rightful Place* by Noel Pearson $27.99
- ☐ **QE 56** *Clivosaurus* by Guy Rundle $27.99
- ☐ **QE 57** *Dear Life* by Karen Hitchcock $27.99
- ☐ **QE 58** *Blood Year* by David Kilcullen $27.99
- ☐ **QE 59** *Faction Man* by David Marr $27.99
- ☐ **QE 60** *Political Amnesia* by Laura Tingle $27.99
- ☐ **QE 61** *Balancing Act* by George Megalogenis $27.99
- ☐ **QE 62** *Firing Line* by James Brown $27.99
- ☐ **QE 63** *Enemy Within* by Don Watson $27.99
- ☐ **QE 64** *The Australian Dream* by Stan Grant $27.99
- ☐ **QE 65** *The White Queen* by David Marr $27.99
- ☐ **QE 66** *The Long Goodbye* by Anna Krien $27.99
- ☐ **QE 67** *Moral Panic 101* by Benjamin Law $27.99
- ☐ **QE 68** *Without America* by Hugh White $27.99

QUARTERLY ESSAY BACK ISSUES

- ☐ **QE 69** *Moment of Truth* by Mark McKenna $27.99
- ☐ **QE 70** *Dead Right* by Richard Denniss $27.99
- ☐ **QE 71** *Follow the Leader* by Laura Tingle $27.99
- ☐ **QE 72** *Net Loss* by Sebastian Smee $27.99
- ☐ **QE 73** *Australia Fair* by Rebecca Huntley $27.99
- ☐ **QE 74** *The Prosperity Gospel* by Erik Jensen $27.99
- ☐ **QE 75** *Men at Work* by Annabel Crabb $27.99
- ☐ **QE 76** *Red Flag* by Peter Hartcher $27.99
- ☐ **QE 77** *Cry Me a River* by Margaret Simons $27.99
- ☐ **QE 78** *The Coal Curse* by Judith Brett $27.99
- ☐ **QE 79** *The End of Certainty* by Katharine Murphy $27.99
- ☐ **QE 80** *The High Road* by Laura Tingle $27.99
- ☐ **QE 81** *Getting to Zero* by Alan Finkel $27.99
- ☐ **QE 82** *Exit Strategy* by George Megalogenis $27.99
- ☐ **QE 83** *Top Blokes* by Lech Blaine $27.99
- ☐ **QE 84** *The Reckoning* by Jess Hill $27.99
- ☐ **QE 85** *Not Waving, Drowning* by Sarah Krasnostein $27.99
- ☐ **QE 86** *Sleepwalk to War* by Hugh White $27.99
- ☐ **QE 87** *Uncivil Wars* by Waleed Aly & Scott Stephens $27.99
- ☐ **QE 88** *Lone Wolf* by Katharine Murphy $27.99
- ☐ **QE 89** *The Wires That Bind* by Saul Griffith $27.99
- ☐ **QE 90** *Voice of Reason* by Megan Davis $27.99
- ☐ **QE 91** *Lifeboat* by Micheline Lee $27.99
- ☐ **QE 92** *The Great Divide* by Alan Kohler $27.99
- ☐ **QE 93** *Bad Cop* by Lech Blaine $27.99
- ☐ **QE 94** *Highway to Hell* by Joëlle Gergis $27.99
- ☐ **QE 95** *High Noon* by Don Watson $27.99
- ☐ **QE 96** *Minority Report* by George Megalogenis $27.99
- ☐ **QE 97** *Losing It* by Jess Hill $29.99
- ☐ **QE 98** *Hard New World* by Hugh White $29.99
- ☐ **QE 99** *Woodside vs the Planet* by Marian Wilkinson $29.99

Order back issues online

Prices include GST.
$10 flat-rate shipping within Australia.
Please include this form with delivery and payment details overleaf.
Back issues also available as ebooks from ebook retailers.

CELEBRATING 100 ISSUES OF QUARTERLY ESSAY

☐ **ONE-YEAR PRINT AND DIGITAL SUBSCRIPTION: $99.99**

- Save nearly $20 off the cover price
- Print edition
- Free home delivery
- Automatically renewing
- Full digital access to all past issues
- App for Android and iPhone users
- ebook files

DELIVERY AND PAYMENT DETAILS

DELIVERY DETAILS:

NAME:

ADDRESS:

EMAIL: PHONE:

PAYMENT DETAILS: Enclose a cheque/money order made out to Schwartz Books Pty Ltd.
Or debit my credit card (MasterCard, Visa and Amex accepted).
Freepost: Quarterly Essay, Reply Paid 90094, Collingwood VIC 3066
All prices include GST, postage and handling.

CARD NO.

EXPIRY DATE: / CCV: AMOUNT: $

PURCHASER'S NAME: SIGNATURE:

Subscribe online at **quarterlyessay.com/subscribe** • Freecall: 1800 077 514 • Phone: 03 9486 0288
Email: subscribe@quarterlyessay.com (please do not send electronic scans of this form)

WANT THE LATEST FROM QUARTERLY ESSAY?

Subscribe to the Friends of Quarterly Essay email newsletter to share in news, updates, events and special offers.